ReWrite

a musical comedy
triple feature

by Joe Iconis

A SAMUEL FRENCH ACTING EDITION

NEW YORK HOLLYWOOD LONDON TORONTO
SAMUELFRENCH.COM

Book and Lyrics Copyright © 2011 by Joe Iconis

ALL RIGHTS RESERVED

Cover Illustraion by Wes Simpkins

CAUTION: Professionals and amateurs are hereby warned that *REWRITE* is subject to a Licensing Fee. It is fully protected under the copyright laws of the United States of America, the British Commonwealth, including Canada, and all other countries of the Copyright Union. All rights, including professional, amateur, motion picture, recitation, lecturing, public reading, radio broadcasting, television and the rights of translation into foreign languages are strictly reserved. In its present form the play is dedicated to the reading public only.

The amateur and professional live stage performance rights to *REWRITE* are controlled exclusively by Samuel French, Inc., and royalty arrangements and licenses must be secured well in advance of presentation. PLEASE NOTE that amateur royalty fees are set upon application in accordance with your producing circumstances. When applying for a royalty quotation and license please give us the number of performances intended, dates of production, your seating capacity and admission fee. Royalties are payable one week before the opening performance of the play to Samuel French, Inc., at 45 W. 25th Street, New York, NY 10010.

Royalty of the required amount must be paid whether the play is presented for charity or gain and whether or not admission is charged.

Stock royalty quoted upon application to Samuel French, Inc.

For all other rights than those stipulated above, apply to: William Morris Endeavor Entertainment, LLC 1325 Avenue of the Americas, New York, NY 10019; attn: Val Day.

Particular emphasis is laid on the question of amateur or professional readings, permission and terms for which must be secured in writing from Samuel French, Inc.

Copying from this book in whole or in part is strictly forbidden by law, and the right of performance is not transferable.

Whenever the play is produced the following notice must appear on all programs, printing and advertising for the play: "Produced by special arrangement with Samuel French, Inc."

Due authorship credit must be given on all programs, printing and advertising for the play.

ISBN 978-0-573-69753-1   Printed in U.S.A.   #29195

No one shall commit or authorize any act or omission by which the copyright of, or the right to copyright, this play may be impaired.

No one shall make any changes in this play for the purpose of production.

Publication of this play does not imply availability for performance. Both amateurs and professionals considering a production are strongly advised in their own interests to apply to Samuel French, Inc., for written permission before starting rehearsals, advertising, or booking a theatre.

No part of this book may be reproduced, stored in a retrieval system, or transmitted in any form, by any means, now known or yet to be invented, including mechanical, electronic, photocopying, recording, videotaping, or otherwise, without the prior written permission of the publisher.

RENTAL MATERIALS

An orchestration consisting of **Piano/Vocal Score** will be loaned two months prior to the production ONLY on the receipt of the Licensing Fee quoted for all performances, the rental fee and a refundable deposit.

Please contact Samuel French for perusal of the music materials as well as a performance license application.

IMPORTANT BILLING AND CREDIT REQUIREMENTS

All producers of *REWRITE* must give credit to the Author of the Play in all programs distributed in connection with performances of the Play, and in all instances in which the title of the Play appears for the purposes of advertising, publicizing or otherwise exploiting the Play and/or a production. The name of the Author *must* appear on a separate line on which no other name appears, immediately following the title and *must* appear in size of type not less than fifty percent of the size of the title type.

In addition the following credit must be given in all programs and publicity information distributed in association with this piece:

REWRITE, a musical comedy triple feature **by Joe Iconis received its World Premiere at URBAN STAGES 2008-2009 Frances Hill, Artistic Director in association with Sara Katz**

REWRITE, a musical comedy triple feature by Joe Iconis, received its world premiere as part of Urban Stages' (Frances Hill, Artistic Director, in association with Sara Katz) 2008-2009 season, opening on December 10, 2008. The production was directed by John Simpkins, with musical direction by Matt Hinkley. The set was by Michael Schweikardt, with costumes by Michelle Eden Humphrey, lighting by Chris Dallos, sound by Craig Kaufman, and video by Alex Koch,. The production stage manager was Carol A. Sullivan, with Theresa Flanagan. The managing director was Lauren Schmiedel. The cast was as follows:

NELSON DRUCKER, THE SLICK DUDE,

    THE PRODUCER .... Nick Blaemire
ASHLEY, A SLUT, THE GIRL BEHIND THE COUNTER .... Badia Farha
MRS. THURSER, THE WOMAN (MISS MARZIPAN), MOM .... Lorinda Lisitza
JENNY VECHARELLI, ANOTHER SLUT,

    THE LADY CUSTOMER .... Lauren Marcus
IKE McCAULEY, THE YOUNG MAN, MICK .... A.J. Shively
THE VOICE, THE WRITER .... Jason "SweetTooth" Williams

REWRITE was subsequently developed at Goodspeed Opera House's (Michael Price, Artistic Director; Bob Alwine, Donna Lynn Hilton; Associate Artistic Directors) Festival of New Musicals, 2010. The production was directed by John Simpkins, with musical direction by Robert Rokicki. The cast was as follows:

IKE McCAULEY, THE YOUNG MAN, MICK .... Seth Eliser
JENNY VECHARELLI, ANOTHER SLUT,

    THE LADY CUSTOMER .... Alexandra Ferrara
ASHLEY, A SLUT, THE GIRL BEHIND

    THE COUNTER .... Stephanie Genovese
MRS. THURSER, THE WOMAN (MISS MARZIPAN),

    MOM .... Stephanie Killough
NELSON DRUCKER, THE SLICK DUDE, FAN BOY ..... Patrick Morrissey
THE VOICE, THE WRITER .... Jason "SweetTooth" Williams

CHARACTERS

The show is performed with a cast of six: three men and three women, all of whom triple specific parts.

MAN 1: Nelson Drucker, The Slick Dude, Fan Boy
MAN 2: Ike McCauley, The Young Man, Mick Jagger
MAN 3: The Voice, The Writer

WOMAN 1: Jenny Veccharelli, A Slut, The Lady Costumer
WOMAN 2: Mrs. Thurser, Miss Marzipan, Mom
WOMAN 3: Ashley, Another Slut, The Girl Behind The Counter

SPECIAL THANKS

Katrina Rose Dideriksen, Ray Munoz, Morgan Pate, Lance Rubin, Jared Weiss, Ars Nova, Ian Kagey, Joe's entire wonderful family, and Jeff Rubin (a good man).

AUTHOR'S NOTE

ReWrite was greatly inspired by the song "All My Little Words" by The Magnetic Fields.

ReWrite *is dedicated to J.V. and all that she stands for.*

MINI-MUSICAL #1

NELSON ROCKS!

CHARACTERS

NELSON DRUCKER
JENNY VECCHARELLI
IKE MCCAULEY
MRS. THURSER
ASHLEY
THE VOICE

(A hallway of lockers at Lowe High.)

NELSON. It's 9:03 on April 23rd and I, Nelson Drucker, am going to ask Jenny Veccharelli to the Junior prom right now.

(He doesn't move.)

I'm gonna ask her right now.

THE FIRST TIME I MET JENNY WAS IN KINDERGARTEN
ALL THE KIDS WERE CALLING ME DRUCKER-SUCKER
BUT JENNY DIDN'T TAKE PART AND
FROM THAT MOMENT I KNEW SHE WAS SPECIAL –
  DIFFERENT, LIKE ME
I KNOW, I KNOW, I KNOW THAT WE ARE MADE FOR EACH
  OTHER
I JUST HOPE THAT JENNY WILL AGREE

*(**JENNY** [16] appears. She giggles.)*

Look at her, she's so hot.

(A school bell rings.)

THE VOICE. Attention students. That was the five minute bell. There is now less than five minutes left to the beginning of period three.

NELSON.
SHE'S TOO GOOD FOR ME
I'M DUNGEONS AND DRAGONS, SHE'S HOMECOMING QUEEN
WE'D LOOK FUNNY TOGETHER
SHE'S FULLY DEVELOPED, I'M IN BETWEEN

BUT I STILL THINK IT COULD WORK, AT LEAST FOR ONE
  DAY, ONE NIGHT, ONE DANCE
IF SHE'D ONLY GIVE ME THE CHANCE

JENNY VECCHARELLI CAN'T YOU SEE I WANT TO HOLD YOU
  TIGHT?
JENNY V. SAY YES TO ME AND THEN WE'LL BE TOGETHER ON
  PROM NIGHT

(**NELSON** *takes a deep breath and begins to walk over to* **JENNY**. **MRS. THURSER** *comes rushing out of her classroom with a stack of papers.*)

MRS. THURSER. Nelson, you owe me three homeworks and the marking period is almost up.

NELSON. I'm sorry, Mrs. Thurser, I'll get them to you by tomorrow at the very latest.

MRS. THURSER. I don't want to have to drop you a letter grade but I will. I'm a strong woman, Nelson. A very strong woman.

NELSON. Tomorrow, I promise.

MRS. THURSER. Something smells like muffins to me. Is somebody making muffins?

(**MRS. THURSER** *leaves and* **NELSON** *makes a beeline for* **JENNY**. *She startles him and he sneezes inwardly.*)

NELSON. *(through a sneeze)* Hi.

JENNY. Oh, hey.

(**JENNY** *smiles.* **NELSON** *smiles. Awkward silence.*)

NELSON. Yeah, sorry, I've got bad allergies, asthma…my inhaler is around somewhere, I had this skateboard instructor once – I skateboard – did you know that I skateboard? – who taught me how to sneeze *in*, which is cool, cuz I never have to worry about buying tissues.

JENNY. That sounds fun!

NELSON. Nah.

(**JENNY** *smiles. Awkward silence.*)

THE VOICE. Four minutes left.

JENNY. Ah, I gotta jet.

NELSON. Ok – Bye, Jenny.

JENNY. Bye, uh…

NELSON. Nelson – Nelson Drucker?

JENNY. Right, right, Nelson.

NELSON. Yeah, I work the lighting board for the musical? I've only worked, like, the last five shows or whatever, so…

JENNY. No, sure, I know. *(pause)* Oh, bye.

NELSON. Sure, cool, bye, Jenny.

(JENNY leaves.)

Oh, she Likes me!

JENNY VECCHARELLI CAN'T YOU SEE I WANT TO HOLD YOU TIGHT?

JENNY V. SAY YES TO ME AND THEN WE'LL BE TOGETHER ON PROM NIGHT

(IKE [17] bumps into NELSON.)

IKE. Yo, Druck-Fuck. Sup, dog?

NELSON. Ike, man, what's going on?

IKE. Did you just say "man" to me?

NELSON. I guess.

IKE. Dude, when you say "man" it sounds forced.

NELSON. Sorry.

IKE. S'all good, bro. I'm just giving you a heads up. That way you won't say it front of anyone who's gonna give you shit about it.

NELSON. Thanks, Ike.

THE VOICE. Attention, will Nelson Drucker please report to the Nurse's office to pick up his IBD medication?

NELSON. *(trying to ignore it)* So what did you want to ask me?

THE VOICE. *(overlapping)* Repeat: will Nelson Drucker please report to the Nurse's office: Nelson, your Irritable Bowel Disorder medication needs picking up immediately. Thank you.

NELSON. Whatever, what did you want some money for lunch or something?

IKE. OK, so tell me, Shit Boy, have you taken Mr. Dodds' test yet?

THE VOICE. Three minutes left.

NELSON. Nah, I'm taking it now.

IKE. Ah. Well, I had LAX practice last night 'till like 7, so what do you say you hook me up with some answers and shit during fourth period?

NELSON. Yeah, sure thing.

IKE. *(like, "Thanks, dude!")* You're my *bitch*, yo!

NELSON. No problem, man.

IKE. Ah?

NELSON. No problem, Ike.

IKE. Much un-gayer.

THE VOICE. Two minutes left.

NELSON. Yeah, you know what, I'm actually in kind of a rush.

IKE. Oh, you're in a *rush?* Sorry, where are you *Rush*ing to?

NELSON. I gotta go ask Veccharelli something.

IKE. Oh. Well I'll come with, I gotta ask her something too.

NELSON. Well, it's kind of, like, personal.

IKE. How could it be personal, she doesn't even know you.

NELSON. Yeah, she does, she knows me.

IKE. Wait, wait, wait, you're not like asking her out are you? *(laughing)*

NELSON. Well I just thought that with prom coming up that maybe I'd ask her.

IKE. You just thought? You thought? Well maybe if you spent a little less time thinking and a little more time not being so gay, she'd say yes to you, but as it happens – she's gonna say 'no.'

NELSON. You don't know that, man. Ike. I mean, you don't know that, Ike.

IKE.

HEY HEY HEY HEY OH OH OH
SHE GONNA SAY SAY SAY SAY
NO NO NO NO

HEY HEY HEY HEY OH OH OH THERE JUSTA
AIN'T NO WAY
SHE GONNA GO OH OH

(laughing) Not gonna happen, Drucker.

NELSON. Well, whatever. I'm still gonna try.

IKE. Yeah, you know what? I think you should. I think you should try, Buddy.

NELSON. And, ya know, she might say yes.

IKE.
> SHE MIGHT SAY YES

NELSON.
> SHE MIGHT SAY YES

IKE.
> SHE MIGHT SAY YES

NELSON.
> SHE MIGHT SAY YES

IKE. Yeah. Well…not if I ask her first.

THE VOICE. One minute left.

NELSON. What does that mean?

IKE. Dude – this is some on-your-mark-get-set-go-shit I'm talking about. You game?

NELSON. Yeah, I guess.

IKE. All right then. On your mark.

NELSON. *(nervous)* Uhhh.

IKE. Get set…

NELSON.
> JENNY V. SAY YES TO ME

IKE. Go!

*(**NELSON** and **IKE** run through the halls.)*

NELSON.
> RUNING, RACING, DARTING, BREATHING
> HEAVY, FEELING SICK AND I'M
> GOING, FLOWING, LOCKERS CLANGING,
> BANGING, RUNNING OUT OF TIME
> PEOPLE, 'SCUSE ME, NOTEBOOKS, LOOSELEAF, PUSHING,
>   SHOVING, BREAKING THROUGH
> AND GOING, GETTING, SNEAKERS, SWEATING
> SCREECHING, TEACHERS, TRYING TO ESCAPE BUT GETTING
>   DRYER, PALER

*(**NELSON** starts wheezing.)*

NELSON.
>WHERE'D I PUT MY DAMN INHALER?
>GOING, BUT NOT FEELING BETTER THERE SHE IS, I LOVE HER DIMPLES
>PULSING, RACING, COLLAR WETTER
>HEART BEAT, SEIZURE, NERVOUS PIMPLES
>
>JENNY
>JENNY
>
>*(NELSON's throat goes dry.)*

NELSON. *(wheezing)* JEHNNY I GAHT SOMETHEEENG TO AHSK YOU.

THE VOICE. Nelson Drucker – we know that you splooged all over the computer keyboard in private study room 3. Please clean it up immediately.

*(Moment of stunned silence. **IKE** pushes **NELSON** out of the way.)*

IKE. Yo, Veccharelli, what do you say you go to prom with me?

JENNY. Prom? You wanna go to prom with me?

IKE. Kinda.

JENNY. OK.

IKE. Phat.

(They hug.)

IKE. *(noticing **NELSON**)* A little space, Gay-Man?

JENNY. Oh, Ike, you're such a funny guy.

*(**IKE** and **JENNY** walk off.)*

NELSON.
>IT'S OVER
>
>*(Lights fade to black. A mournful moment. Lights up on **NELSON**.)*

NELSON. It's 9:03am, on April 23rd and I, Nelson Drucker am going to ask Jenny Veccharelli to the Junior prom right now.

(a bell rings)

THE VOICE. Attention, students, that was the five minute bell. You have five minutes to get to class.

(JENNY appears at her locker. She giggles.)

Look at her.

I'M NOT COOL ENOUGH FOR HER
I WEAR A RETAINER AND MAKE COMPUTERS FROM PARTS
I'M A GEEK AND SHE'S NOT, I'M SUCH A FREAK, SHE'S SO HOT
SHE WEARS BABY-DOLL TEES AND DOTS HER 'I'S WITH HEARTS

JENNY VECCHARELLI...

IKE. *(interrupting)* Yo, Druck-Fuck. Sup, Dog?

NELSON. Ike, man, what's going on?

IKE. Did you just say "man" to me?

NELSON. *Yes.* I did. *(a pause)* That cool?

IKE. Yeah, sure, whatever. Listen – I need answers to the Dodds' test. I was wondering if you could hook me up during fourth period.

THE VOICE. Four minutes left.

NELSON. Yeah, surething, but listen – I gotta go cuz I'm in a bit of a ru – *(stops himself)* – I sort of have to take care of something. Something important.

IKE. You have to take care of something? Oh, gee sorry, I didn't realize that raping little boys was a pressing matter.

THE VOICE. *(overlapping)* Attention students: just a quick announcement to inform you all that Lowe High's very own Nelson Drucker has been named Computer Shooter Magazine's hacker of the year. Congratulations Nelson, and keep up the good work.

(JENNY walks past.)

JENNY. Congratulations, Nelson.

(**NELSON** *smiles.* **JENNY** *passes.*)

NELSON. I *rock.*
JENNY V CONGRATULATED ME WHICH MEANS I THINK SHE MIGHT AGREE IT'S DESTINY THAT WE SHOULD BE TOGETHER ON PROM NIGHT

IKE. Oh, snap, did the Vec leave?

NELSON. Yeah she went...

(*Light bulb.* **NELSON** *points* **IKE** *in the wrong direction.*)

That way.

(**IKE** *heads off after her.*)

IKE. Remember – fourth period.

NELSON. Right, sure – fourth period, I'll be there.

(**MRS. THURSER** *comes rushing out of her classroom with a stack of papers.* **NELSON** *tries to get past her, but she keeps blocking his way.*)

MRS. THURSER. Nelson, you owe me three homeworks and the marking period is almost up.

NELSON. Sorry, Mrs. Thurser, you'll get them tomorrow.

MRS. THURSER. I don't want to have to drop you a letter grade but I will. I'm a strong woman, Nelson. A very strong woman.

NELSON. Tomorrow! See ya!

(**MRS. THURSER** *physically halts* **NELSON** *with her hand, as if she has to tell him The Most Important Thing Of All Time.*)

MRS. THURSER. Something smells like muffins to me. Is somebody making muffins?

(**MRS. THURSER** *leaves and* **JENNY** *taps* **NELSON** *on the shoulder. He sneezes inwardly.*)

JENNY. What was that?

NELSON. Sorry. I just sneezed in.

(*long pause*)

JENNY. That's so cool.

NELSON. Thanks, it's nothing really.

JENNY. Well, listen, I just wanted to say congratulations. I've always known you were an awesome guy, and I'm just glad that Computer Shooter Magazine finally agrees with me.

NELSON. You read Computer Shooter?

(**JENNY** *makes the international "shhh" sign.*)

NELSON. No way…You're totally lying. You're lying to me.

JENNY. I'm no liar, Nelson, lying's not boss. Not boss at all.

NELSON. No, I'm not calling you a liar, I'm just a little surprised. I mean, I didn't even think you knew who I was and then you come up and start talking about computers, and being nice to me…It's just kinda, ya know, a little X-Files-y, that's all.

JENNY. Oh, Nelson, you're such a funny guy!

NELSON. Yeah, sure, that's me, I'm a funny guy.

THE VOICE. Three minutes left.

NELSON. *(overlapping)* Three minutes left 'till class.

JENNY. Ohmygosh, is that a "Star Trek" watch?

NELSON. No.

JENNY. Yes it is.

NELSON. It is a "Star Trek" watch, but it's only cuz my "Speed Racer" watch is in the shop.

JENNY. *(overlapping)* Nelson, Nelson – don't be ashamed of it. I think it's…

(**JENNY** *makes the international "I've Been Naughty" face.*)

NELSON. What?

JENNY.
> NOTHING GETS ME HOT LIKE STAR TREK, BABY
> THAT SPACE SHIT IS SEXY AS HELL
> JUST THE SIGHT OF A TRIBBLE OR A KLINGON BRINGS ON
>   NOTIONS OF EMOTIONS TOO BLUE TO TELL

NELSON. Whoa, whoa, you're getting a little carried away there.

JENNY. *(overlapping)*
YEAH, YEAH, YEAH
NOTHING GETS ME HOT LIKE STAR TREK BABY, COME ON!

*(**NELSON** is shocked and starts to wheeze. **JENNY** thinks he's panting and begins to breathe heavily. This continues for a moment.)*

NELSON. Juhst a scheck…

*(**NELSON** pulls out his inhaler.)*

JENNY.
NOTHING'S QUITE AS RAD AS ASHTMA, BABY
IT'S AS COOL AS LUNG DISORDERS CAN BE
THERE'S SOMETHING KINDA CRIMINAL 'BOUT TAKING HITS
    OFF AN INHALER
THAT APPEALS TO THE BAD GIRL IN ME
YEAH YEAH NOTHING'S QUITE AS RAD AS ASTHMA, BABY,
    C'MON!

NELSON. Wait, wait, wait – why are you saying this?

JENNY. What do you mean?

NELSON. Are you, like, making fun of me? Cuz what you're saying – it seems a little weird.

JENNY.
WE'RE JUST TWO PEOPLE TALKING
WE'RE JUST TWO PEOPLE TALKING
WE'RE JUST TWO PEOPLE TALKING
TO EACH OTHER
WHAT'S WEIRD ABOUT

TWO PEOPLE TALKING
WE'RE JUST TWO PEOPLE TALKING
WE'RE JUST TWO PEOPLE TALKING
TO EACH OTHER

BOTH.
WHAT'S WEIRD ABOUT
TWO PEOPLE TALKING
TWO PEOPLE TALKING
TWO PEOPLE TALKING
TO EACH OTHER

BOTH.
> WHAT'S WEIRD ABOUT
> TWO PEOPLE SMILING
> TWO PEOPLE LAUGHING
> TWO PEOPLE TALKING

IKE. *(interrupting)* Yo, Veccharelli, I gotta ask you something.

THE VOICE. Two minutes left.

JENNY. Actually, Ike, I was talking to Nelson.

NELSON. Yeah, and besides, I wanted to ask her something.

JENNY. You want to Ask me something?

IKE. I just need you for a sec.

(IKE starts pulling JENNY away.)

NELSON. Ike, why don't you, ya know…

IKE. *(overlap)* Dude, leave, I gotta speak to the Vec.

JENNY. I was talking to Nelson, Ike.

IKE. Stop being such a Vag-face, Veccharelli, I wanna ask you something, I said.

NELSON. Yo, don't talk to her like that.

IKE. Like what? What I did I say?

NELSON. Ike, get the hell out of here – just back off.

IKE. Or what?

NELSON. Or, I'm gonna make you back off.

IKE. The hell does that mean?

JENNY. Nelson, don't!

NELSON. Stay outta this, Jenny.

THE VOICE. One minute left.

IKE. I'd like to see you try, Pube-Sucker. Go ahead, take your best shot.

(NELSON whips out his inhaler and sprays IKE in the eyes.)

IKE. *Ah!* My eyes are blind like a blind man! Damn you, Nelson Drucker! Damn You!

(IKE stumbles off-stage, screaming.)

NELSON.
 JENNY
 JENNY

THE VOICE. Pardon me, but will Nelson Drucker please report to the nurse's office to pick up his IBD medication. Nelson – the medication to help alleviate the stress on your back caused by your Insanely Big Dick needs picking up immediately. Thank you.

(a beat)

NELSON. *(You slick fella, you)* Where was I?
 JENNY I GOT SOMETHING TO ASK YOU
 Jenny…would you like…like to go to prom with me?

JENNY. Well… *(long pause)* Yes.

JENNY/NELSON/IKE. *(ad. lib)*
 YES
 YES
 SHE SAID YES, MY GOD SHE SAID YES, YEAH

NELSON. I can't believe it, I never thought this would happen.

JENNY. I can't believe it either.

NELSON. I'm gonna call my mom. I'm gonna call her and tell her that Jenny Veccharelli is going to the prom with me. This is so cool!

JENNY. *(overlapping)* Nelson, Nelson, Nelson, don't get so excited.

NELSON. Why? Why shouldn't I be excited?

JENNY. Because you haven't actually asked me yet.

NELSON. What are you talking about? I just did.

THE VOICE. No, Nelson, Jenny's right. You've just been imagining all of this. The last twelve minutes have all taken place in your head.

NELSON. In my head? So none of this actually happened?

JENNY. Sorry.

NELSON. What about when you said yes to me?

THE VOICE. In your head.

NELSON. What about when you said yes to Ike?

THE VOICE. In your head.

NELSON. So I haven't asked you yet?

JENNY. Not in real life, no. But you're going to now.

NELSON. I am?

THE VOICE. You've been standing at your locker for the last twelve minutes thinking about it, for shit's sake, of course you're gonna ask her!

NELSON. I am. Are you gonna say yes?

JENNY.
I MIGHT SAY YES

NELSON.
YOU MIGHT SAY YES

THE VOICE.
SHE MIGHT SAY YES

NELSON.
YOU MIGHT SAY YES

JENNY. Or I might say 'no.' But I guess there's only one to find out.

NELSON. I guess.

THE VOICE. C'mon, boyo – she's at her locker right now. March on over there and give 'er what's for!

JENNY. You can do it, Nelson. Be a tiger: go, go, go, go...

THE VOICE/JENNY. Go, go, go, go!

NELSON. It's 9:03 am, on April 23rd and I, Nelson Drucker am going to ask Jenny Veccharelli to the Junior prom right now.

(A bell rings.)

THE VOICE. Attention students, that was your five minute bell.

NELSON.
THE 23RD OF APRIL
NINE O'THREE
I'M READY, I'M READY, I'M READY TO GO
OH, JENNY, GET READY FOR ME

NELSON. *(cont.)*
>OK, NELSON, REMEMBER YOUR BREATHING
>BE ILL, BUT CHILL, BE CALM
>IT'S NINE O'THREE AND I WON'T WAIT A MINUTE MORE AND
>BY THE TIME THE CLOCK IS CHIMING NINE O'FOUR
>I'LL BE DEEP IN CONVERSATION WITH THE GIRL I ADORE
>THEN I'M GONNA ASK JENNY TO PROM

MRS. THURSER. Nelson, you owe me three homeworks and the marking period is almost up.

NELSON. I'm sorry, Mrs. Thurser, I'll get them to you by tomorrow.

MRS. THURSER. I don't want to have to drop you a letter grade but I will. I'm a strong woman, Nelson. A very strong woman.

NELSON. Tomorrow, definitely!

MRS. THURSER. Something smells like muffins to me. Is somebody making muffins?

JENNY. Oh, that's me! Everyone always tells me that I smell like muffins!

MRS. THURSER. *(A great secret has been unlocked.)* Thank You. Thank you for telling me that.

(MRS. THURSER runs off.)

JENNY. Hi, Nelson.

NELSON. Hey. Jenny.

(IKE grabs NELSON.)

IKE. Hey, Druck-Fuck, I forgot to ask you, you take the Dodd's test yet?

(IKE notices JENNY.)

Hey.

(JENNY smiles.)

You're Jenny Veccharelli right?

(JENNY smiles, embarrassed.)

I'm Ike.

JENNY. I know.

NELSON. I help him out from time to time.

IKE. Oh, oh, oh, oh. *Bitch*, just fork over the answers.

JENNY. *(to herself)* So grody.

NELSON. Sure, man.

IKE. Did you just call me 'man'?

THE VOICE. Four minutes left.

IKE. Ah, listen, it was cool talking to you, Jenny. We should maybe hang sometime. My mom had this big book party a couple days ago, so the fridge is, like, full of wine-in-the-box. We could have some fun.

(**JENNY** *smiles.* **IKE** *leaves.*)

JENNY. I've totally talked to him like a thousand times and he doesn't remember.

IKE.
SHE'S KINDA HOT
WHY DIDN'T I EVER NOTICE IT BEFORE?

JENNY. He must've been high or something every time we spoke.

NELSON. *(laughs)* Yeah, right?

IKE.
MUST'VE BEEN HIGH
CUZ I NEVER NOTICED HER BEFORE

I USUALLY GO FOR MORE OF A HO
BUT THERE'S SOMETHING 'BOUT JENNY I DIG
SHE'S NOT A SLUT BUT SHE'S HOT, SHE'S AN ANGEL YET
  SHE'S NOT
YEAH THERE'S SOMETHING 'BOUT JENNY I DIG

JENNY. Hey, listen, I just wanted to tell you that I think you're doing such an awesome job on the musical.

NELSON. OK.

THE VOICE. Three minutes left.

JENNY. Yeah, I was just talking to Margaret about it, and we were saying that you're, like, the best lighting board operator ever.

NELSON. OK.

JENNY. Yeah, and, you're only a Junior so, that's like, pretty incredible. Oh my god, how cold is it in this school – my nips are totally Empire Stating.

IKE.
SHE'S THE KIND OF BITCH THAT YOU CAN TAKE HOME TO MOM

NELSON.
SHE'S FAT GIRL NICE BUT HER BOD IS THE BOMB

NELSON/IKE.
I GOTTA ASK JENNY TO PROM
I'M GONNA ASK JENNY TO PROM
I'M GONNA ASK JENNY TO PROM

NELSON. Speaking of the musical, you're really good in it, ya know.

JENNY. Shut up. I didn't get the part I wanted but, whatever right? I mean, between Home and Careers and Key Club, I gotta lot on my plate.

THE VOICE. Two minutes left.

NELSON. I'm busy, too.

JENNY. What's does your shirt say?

NELSON. Uh…It's supposed to say "Evil Dead," but the "L" and the last "D" have worn off so now it just says "Evi Dea."

JENNY. Nelson, you're so funny. You're really a funny guy. (*JENNY burps.*) OhmyGod can you smell that?! That's bif-nasty! That's the last time I eat a hameggandcheese from the Caf before class.

(**NELSON** *and* **IKE** *stare at* **JENNY**, *transfixed. They are in love.*)

What?

NELSON/IKE.
JENNY VECCHARELLI CAN'T YOU SEE

IKE.
MY GOD I BET SHE'S TIGHT

BOTH.
JENNY V. SAY YES TO ME AND THEN WE'LL BE TOGETHER ON PROM NIGHT

THE VOICE. Attention students – would Jenny Veccharelli please report to the main office immediately.

JENNY. Oh no. I was supposed to – I had to take care of something. Oh, God, I don't know if I'm gonna make it in time. *(as she's running off)* Bye Nelson! Goodbye!

NELSON/IKE. Jenny!

NELSON. Wait!

NELSON/IKE. I wanted to ask you something!

JENNY. I have to go!

THE VOICE. Attention students – there is now only One Minute Left. Period three will begin in Less Than One Minute!

NELSON/IKE/JENNY.
RUNNING, RACING, DARTING, BREATHING
HEAVY, FEELING SICK AND I'M
GOING, FLOWING, LOCKERS CLANGING,
BANGING, RUNNING OUT OF TIME

IKE/JENNY.
PEOPLE, 'SCUSE ME, NOTEBOOKS, LOOSELEAF
PUSHING, SHOVING, BREAKING THROUGH
AND GOING, GETTING, SNEAKERS, SWEATING
SCREECHING, TEACHERS, TRYING TO

NELSON. JENNY
JENNY VECCHARELLI CAN'T YOU SEE?

JENNY.
RUNING, RACING, DARTING, BREATHING
HEAVY, FEELING SICK AND I'M
GOING, FLOWING, LOCKERS CLANGING,
BANGING, RUNNING OUT OF TIME

NELSON.
JENNY V. OH PLEASE SAY YES TO ME

IKE.
JENNY VECCHARELLI WILL SAY YES TO ME

JENNY.
I GOTTA GO, I GOTTA GO, BECAUSE I CAN'T WASTE ANOTHER
MINUTE I'LL BE LATE FOR CLASS

NELSON/IKE.
>I KNOW I KNOW I KNOW

NELSON.
>THAT WE ARE MADE FOR EACH OTHER

IKE.
>WE'RE GONNA GO WITH EACH OTHER

ALL THREE.
>I KNOW I KNOW I KNOW I GOTTA RUN
>I KNOW I KNOW I KNOW I'M ALMOST DONE
>I CAN SEE THE END, IT SEEMS SO NEAR
>I'M CLOSER, CLOSER, CLOSER,
>I'M CLOSER, CLOSER, CLOSER,
>I'M CLOSER, CLOSER, CLOSER, I'M HERE

(They crash into each other. Screaming/brushing off/ paper flying.)

(ad. lib) Would you watch where you're going? What the scag?

NELSON. Jenny? My glasses!

*(**NELSON** puts his glasses on.)*

NELSON.
>JENNY
>JENNY

THE VOICE. Twenty five seconds left.

NELSON.
>JENNY I GOT SOMETHING TO ASK YOU

Jenny Veccharelli – would you like to go to the prom with me?

(a huge long pause)

JENNY. No.

(a bell rings)

NELSON. What?

JENNY. No. I can't.

IKE. Snap!

JENNY. Ike – could you give us a second?

IKE. Jenny Veccharelli, would you like to go to the prom with me?

JENNY. What?

IKE. Jenny Veccharelli, would you like to go to the prom with me?

JENNY. Are you serious?

IKE. As crabs.

JENNY. Did you even listen to me? I mean, if I'm not gonna go with Nelson why would I go with you?

IKE. Because he's ugly.

JENNY. Well, you smell like ball sweat.

IKE. No I don't.

JENNY. Yes you do. Everyone in the school knows it but no one says anything cuz your dad is dead.

(long pause.)

IKE. *(like "Fuck you")* Point taken.

*(**IKE** leaves.)*

JENNY. What I was saying was: No, I don't want to go to the prom with you.

NELSON. Can you actually *stop* saying that so much, please?

JENNY. *(overlapping)* But, it's not cuz I don't like you. I actually really do. It's just that – I'm sort of seeing someone.

NELSON. You are?

JENNY. Yeah. His name is Matt. He para-sails?

NELSON. Oh. That guy.

JENNY. Seriously, though – if he wasn't, like, *(making quotation mark fingers)* "in the picture," I totally would go with you. You're a good person.

NELSON. I am?

JENNY. Yeah. Some people are just good. I truly believe that.

NELSON. Me too.

JENNY. Ah! Well, that's something we've got in common. *(A moment.)* So, I have to go.

NELSON. Right, right.

JENNY. Yeah, my Mom. She's always on my case if I don't check in during the day. I wanna just be like: "Suck it, I'm a grown up," but I can't cuz she, like, birthed me.

NELSON. Ha…you said "Suck It."

JENNY. You rock, Nelson Drucker.

NELSON. I'm glad you think that is the case.

JENNY. Oh and remember that time that I made quotation mark fingers like a minute ago?

NELSON. Yeah?

JENNY. I apologize, I don't know why I did that. I actually really hate quotation mark fingers. Well, bye!

(*JENNY leaves. NELSON goes to his locker. A **NERDY GIRL** [15] appears. They notice each other and pretend that they don't.*)

NERDY GIRL. Hey – is that an "Evil Dead" shirt?

NELSON. Yeah, it is.

NERDY GIRL. Which one do you like better?

NELSON. Well, "2" is a more gorier movie, but there's something special about "1."

NERDY GIRL. I totally agree.

NELSON. Nelson, by the way.

NERDY GIRL. Ashley. Is my name.

NELSON. Are you a Frosh?

ASHLEY. No, no, I'm a Sophomore, but my bank of lockers is being repainted, so they put me here. (**ASHLEY** *does her famous E.T. impression.*) "Ashley phone home."

NELSON. Ha. E.T. You know, that's so weird that you knew this was an "Evil Dead" shirt cuz, like, not a lot of people have seen that movie. It's weird that you said that to me.

ASHLEY.

WE'RE JUST TWO PEOPLE TALKING
WE'RE JUST TWO PEOPLE TALKING
WE'RE JUST TWO PEOPLE TALKING
TO EACH OTHER
WHAT'S WEIRD ABOUT

NELSON.
>TWO PEOPLE TALKING
>TWO PEOPLE TALKING
>TWO PEOPLE TALKING
>TO EACH OTHER

NELSON/ASHLEY.
>WE'RE JUST
>TWO PEOPLE TALKING
>TWO PEOPLE TALKING
>TWO PEOPLE TALKING
>TO EACH OTHER
>
>WE'RE JUST
>TWO PEOPLE SMILING
>TWO PEOPLE LAUGHING
>TWO PEOPLE TALKING

(a bell rings)

THE VOICE. Attention students: the new period has begun. Please report to your classes immediately.

NELSON. So, I guess, I'll see you around.

ASHLEY. I hope so.

NELSON. Bye, Ashley.

ASHLEY. Bye, Nelson.

NELSON. *I rock!*

The End

MINI-MUSICAL #2

MISS MARZIPAN

CHARACTERS

THE WOMAN (MISS MARZIPAN)
THE YOUNG MAN
SLICK DUDE
A SLUT
ANOTHER SLUT
THE VOICE

(A suburban kitchen. There is a table and counter, an oven, fridge, and a cupboard. **THE WOMAN** *is buzzing around the kitchen and crazily mixing things in bowls. She is clearly preparing for some kind of party. She looks frazzled but happy and not-at-all insane. No, not even a little bit. Of course not.)*

THE WOMAN.

STIR THE EGGS AND BEAT THE FLOUR
SORTA SMELL, BUT SCREW THE SHOWER
ONLY HAVE A HALF AN HOUR
'TILL BIG D ARRIVES FOR DINNER
RUSHING, RUSHING, RUSHING, RUSH

NO TIME FOR CLEANING SPILLS OR STOPPING
WHIZ THE FIZZ, AND CHOP THE TOPPING
KNEES ARE BUCKLING, HEART IS POPPING
THINKING 'BOUT BIG D FOR DINNER
BLUSHING, BLUSHING, BLUSHING, GUSH

CUZ I HAVEN'T SEEN HIM SINCE HIGH SCHOOL
SINCE HE METAMORPHOSED AND BECAME
A BIG-ASS, BIG DEAL CEO
WHILE I REMAIN THE SAME OLD SAME OLD SAME

I NEED TO BE AS IMPRESSIVE AS I POSSIBLY CAN
SO, THAT'S WHY I'M MAKING MARZIPAN
MAKING MY FAMOUS MARZIPAN

AND HE'S GONNA LOVE IT, LOVE IT, LOVE IT, YEAH!
HE'S GONNA LOVE ME, LOVE ME, LOVE ME, YEAH!
AND HE'LL SEE I'M NOT THE KIND WHO CARES ABOUT WHAT HE'S WORTH
AND HE'LL FORGET ABOUT HIS WIFE WHO DIED IN CHILD BIRTH
AND WE'LL BE TOGETHER, ME AND MY BIG DEAL MAN
AS THE RESULT OF MARZIPAN
THAT'S WHY I'M MAKING MARZIPAN

(We hear some noise coming from the pantry. **THE WOMAN** *clearly hears it too, but she ignores it.)*

THE WOMAN. *(cont.)*

> DOME THE FOAM, INFUSE WITH ALMOND
> CLOCK IS TICKING LIKE A BOMB AND
> BREATHING DEEP, REMAINING CALM AND

(That noise again. This time it's loud enough to stop **THE WOMAN** *dead in her tracks. She ignores it again and resumes.)*

> TIME TO ADD THE COLOR IN
> IT'S ALMOST SIX, IN TWENTY MINUTES
> HE'LL BE HERE AND WE'LL BEGIN
> IT'S GETTING CLOSER, GETTING CLOSER
> RUSHING, RUSHING, RUSHING

(That noise again, this time louder – the door even shakes a little. **THE WOMAN** *can ignore it no longer. She is totally irritated by the noise. She pushes the bowl away and gets up.)*

THE WOMAN. Ugh!

*(***THE WOMAN*** walks over to the pantry and swings open the door. Inside is a* **YOUNG MAN**, *tied to a chair with a gag in his mouth. He has some blood on his face and looks terrified.)*

THE WOMAN. *(screaming)* Do you want me to fucking cut you again, is that what you God Damn want? Shut your Fucking Mouth, Mister!

(She slams the door shut. She composes herself and walks back over to her table as if nothing had happened. She sits back at the bowl. Deep breath. Ahhh.)

And in five minutes, you'll be done, my marzipans. And my life will be fixed. Yay!

> OH, HE'S GONNA LOVE IT, LOVE IT, LOVE IT, YEAH!
> HE'S GONNA LOVE ME, LOVE ME, LOVE ME, YEAH!
> AND HE'LL PROPOSE RIGHT ON THE SPOT BECAUSE HE
>   CAN'T CONTROL

ALL THE LOVE FOR ME THAT'S EATING UP HIS VERY SOUL
AND WE'LL BE TOGETHER, ME AND MY BIG DEAL MAN
AS THE RESULT OF MARZIPAN
THAT'S WHY I'M MAKING MARZI –

(The telephone rings.)

THE WOMAN. *(cont.)* Oh, heck, today! If it's not one thing, dot-dot-dot…

(She answers the phone.)

(singing, practically) Hello? *(dead)* Hi, Mommy. No, I'm not disappointed it's you, honest I'm not, I just thought maybe it was Big D. Big D, from high school? You know – the one who owns the computer company now? Of course you've heard of him, Mommy, he's in Newsday all the time – he was just voted one of Nassau County's top five most famous residents. Susan Lucci. Anyway, he's coming over for a dinner party! Because I'm an attractive woman, that's why. No – don't come over, I don't need your help. I know I'm not married. I know I'm old. Well, maybe a career isn't for me. Maybe I'm not a career type of girl. Yes, I know I'm not a girl anymore. Stop. Just – I just need you to be quiet, ok? *(calming herself down)* Quiet, quiet, quiet, quiet, shhh…

(We hear some loud banging coming from the pantry.)

It was nothing, it's thunder, there's horrible thunder here on Fernwood Terrace, Mommy, I'm surprised you can't hear it from where you are.

(THE WOMAN *picks up a bag of flour and throws it against the Pantry door, which stops moving.)*

I have to go. Just need to take care of one more thing and my house will be perfect. Yes. I know it's technically your house. Love you too. Bye.

(THE WOMAN *hangs up the phone.)*

THE YOUNG MAN. *(muffled; from inside the pantry)* Hey! Open Up! Hey! Please! C'mon! Please!

(THE WOMAN *grabs a huge knife and swings open the pantry door.)*

THE WOMAN. How did you get the gag out of your mouth?

THE YOUNG MAN. I chewed through it, please, let me go take a piss!

THE WOMAN. No way, José, I know what that means, I've seen HBO. You ask to go to the bathroom and then you climb out a window or you craft a shiv out of the end of a toothbrush and use it to murder me. I will not let you murder me.

THE YOUNG MAN. No, I swear, I just gotta piss, please, just let me take a piss, I'm gonna piss all over myself.

THE WOMAN. No!

THE YOUNG MAN.
C'MON
THERE'S A TENSION TENSING UP MY EVERY BONE
A SERRATED, AGITATED TIDAL ZONE
AND IT'S SHARP AND IT'S SQUEEZE
AND I'M BEGING YOU, PLEASE
OH PLEASE LEMME TAKE A PISS

THE WOMAN. And I will *not* continue this conversation if you are insistent on using the P-word. I loathe that word and I won't have it. I'm sorry, I just won't.

(**THE WOMAN** *walks over to her kitchen table, as if playing hard to get.* **THE YOUNG MAN** *moves his chair out of the pantry through a series of lunge-forwards.*)

THE YOUNG MAN. *(trying to be calm, cool, and collected)* I'm sorry? I'm sorry. I said the P-word to sort of emphasize just how severe my situation is. I have a very intolerant bladder and I'm actually in horrible discomfort right now and I don't want to Piss – (**THE WOMAN** *makes a face.*) Pee – (**THE WOMAN** *makes another face.*) Urinate? (**THE WOMAN** *smiles.*) …all over myself, but I'm going to in a second if you don't let me go and I Know that you don't want this kitchen reaking of my urine for your dinner party!

THE WOMAN. *(dawning on her)* You're right. I guess I don't want this kitchen reeking of your urine, but – no! You have to stay like that until after dinner is over, I'm sorry. You will not ruin this for me.

THE YOUNG MAN. Lady, you're the one who kidnapped me!

THE WOMAN. Kidnapped?

THE YOUNG MAN. Kidnapped!

THE WOMAN. Kidnapped?

THE YOUNG MAN. Yes!

THE WOMAN. *(like "Oh, come on!")* Please!

THE YOUNG MAN. Kidnapped!

THE WOMAN. *(like "Oh, come on!")* Oh.

THE YOUNG MAN. I was in the parking lot and you cut me and tied me up and put me in your trunk – kidnapped!

THE WOMAN. Ok, first of all – you know perfectly well, I didn't mean to cut you. I was just trying to scare you but you were moving around so much your face just went into my knife.

THE YOUNG MAN. Let me use the bathroom.

THE WOMAN. Secondly, I didn't mean to *(making quotation mark fingers)* "kidnap" you. I asked you first if you wanted to come to the dinner party.

THE YOUNG MAN. You asked if I wanted to be your son!

THE WOMAN. To pretend, Mr. Literal, to pretend that you were my son!

THE YOUNG MAN. Well, don't you think that's sort of a weird request?

THE WOMAN. I was nervous, I told you, I was nervous. A very impressive man is coming over for dinner. His wife is dead and he has two sons. I thought if I had a son, too, we'd have something to talk about. A conversation starter. Like a coffee table book. I just wanted you to be my coffee table book.

THE YOUNG MAN. Can I please go urinate now?

THE WOMAN. No! Stop asking me that! If you don't stop, I'm gonna…I'm gonna hurt you or something.

THE YOUNG MAN. I don't care.

THE WOMAN. What?

THE YOUNG MAN.
>I DON'T CARE
>I DON'T CARE
>I DON'T CARE ABOUT ANYTHING AT ALL

THE WOMAN. You don't care about getting cut with a knife?

THE YOUNG MAN. Nope.

THE WOMAN. I think getting cut with a knife sounds horrible.

THE YOUNG MAN. I don't care. I can't feel anything, anyway.

THE WOMAN. Of course you can!

THE YOUNG MAN. No. I don't care enough about anything to have feelings. I'm an apathist.

THE WOMAN. That sounds serious. Don't you want to feel something?

THE YOUNG MAN. The world is just messed up. I've seen the way people are towards each other and it sickens me. I'd off myself if I cared enough. I'm an apathist.

THE WOMAN. You need a friend, I think.

THE YOUNG MAN. Listen. You kidnapped the wrong dude, OK? I'm a depressed, supremely fucked-up young man and normally I wouldn't even give a shit that you kidnapped me. But today it just so happens that I have to piss so fuckin bad I think I'm gonna explode.

THE WOMAN. I feel like that too, sometimes! Sometimes I feel like I'm so full of sadness and loneliness that I'm going to blow up like a balloon and just explode! It's so refreshing to hear that someone else feels like me!
>I HAVE SO MUCH LONELINESS INSIDE ME

THE YOUNG MAN. Jesus Christ.

THE WOMAN.
>I CARRY IT WITHIN ME EVERY DAY

THE YOUNG MAN. I cannot fucking believe this.

THE WOMAN.
>BUT NOW THAT YOU ARE SITTING HERE BESIDE ME
>I HOPE THE LONELINESS DECIDES THAT IT'S TIME IT GOES AWAY

THE YOUNG MAN.
  HEY!
  I DON'T CARE
  I DON'T CARE
  I DON'T CARE ABOUT ANYTHING AT ALL

THE WOMAN. Oh! Look at your forehead. You're bleeding still from our little knife accident. Here let me fix it.

(She goes to touch his cut.)

THE YOUNG MAN. *(suddenly explosive)* DON'T YOU TOUCH ME.

THE WOMAN. You snapped at me.

THE YOUNG MAN. Cuz I don't like to be fucking touched by Crazy Fucking Housewives, ok?

THE WOMAN. I'm not a wife. But thank you for thinking that. That's nice of you! He thinks I'm a wife, yet!

*(A pause. **THE YOUNG MAN** notices the TV which has been on mute the whole time.)*

THE WOMAN. Oh! Television? You like it?

*(**THE WOMAN** grabs the remote, un-mutes the TV, and puts the remote on **THE YOUNG MAN**'s lap. We hear **THE VOICE** blare from the TV. It startles **THE YOUNG MAN** who jumps. **THE WOMAN** doesn't flinch.)*

THE VOICE. *(Manic, horrific, Screaming)* Only five minutes left to buy a brand new Muffin Carrier, only $33.33! This is a Home Channel Suburbia Special! Protect your baked goods from the elements, from the hands of children, from people-in-general! Five minutes left! Bang! Five minutes left! Bang! *(**THE VOICE** repeats this on an endless loop.)*

THE WOMAN. *(over top of the "Five Minutes Left" speech)* This is the only channel I get. It's so relaxing.

(Nothing.)

You're very reserved, I like that. Do you have a girlfriend? C'mon, you're no fun!

(She mutes the T.V.)

Do you have a girlfriend?

(Nothing.)

THE WOMAN. *(explosively excited)* Do you have a boyfriend?

*(**THE YOUNG MAN** gives her a "Fuck You" look.)*

THE WOMAN. You could have one if you wanted one. I don't have one, either. I'm between mates. Are you between mates?

(Nothing.)

Every person I talk to makes me feel so bad about myself – like I'm crashing a party or something. I just want someone who makes me feel welcome. That's why I'm so excited about Big D. It's funny – in high school I never even really knew he existed. But now, I'm gonna open my heart to him, Mister. Lay it all on the table. "I'm Lonely, Your wife is dead- Let's Fall In Love!" How could he say no to that!

OH, HE'S GONNA LOVE IT, LOVE IT, LOVE IT, YEAH!
HE'S GONNA LOVE ME, LOVE ME, LOVE ME, YEAH!

*(**THE WOMAN** dances around the kitchen. She sings into whisks, jumps on the table, twirls. That sort of thing.)*

IN TWENTY YEARS WE'LL BE LOUNGING ON A GOLD DEVAN
KISSING, REMINISCING 'BOUT HOW WE BEGAN
JUST ME AND MY BIG DEAL MAN
AS A RESULT OF MARZI –

(In a fit of giddiness, the woman twirls so agressively that she knocks all of her marizpan off the table, slips and lands on the marzipan. It's ruined.)

THE WOMAN. No!

*(**THE WOMAN** tries to pick up the marzipan like an injured baby. She's just making things worse.)*

My marzipans! Ruined! No. No.

*(**THE WOMAN** crumbles to the floor.)*

How could I let this happen? How could I?

*(**THE WOMAN** is a crying mess on the floor. **THE YOUNG MAN** looks at her. He looks at the bathroom door.*

He decides to seize the opportunity. He does his series of lunge-forwards towards the bathroom door. He makes it to the door, which is closed. He tries to open the knob with his teeth. No dice. Shit. He turns back towards **THE WOMAN**.*)*

THE YOUNG MAN. Yo. Yo, you. Just calm down, okay. Woman – just serve some ice cream or something for dessert.

THE WOMAN. And what about the main course, what am I supposed to serve for that?!

THE YOUNG MAN. Well, what did you make for the main course?

THE WOMAN. Marzipan, you fool! I made Appetizer Marzipan, Main Course Marzipan, and Dessert Marzipan. And now? All of it, gone.

THE YOUNG MAN. It's kind of weird to make a whole meal of nothing but marzipan.

THE WOMAN. Well, I made it in the shape of food, for God's Sake – what do you think I am? Big D. What is he going to think of me. You know what? Maybe I better burn the house down to avoid embarrassment.

THE YOUNG MAN. No.

*(***THE WOMAN** *gets up and starts looking for matches.)*

THE WOMAN. Yes, really, I've thought it through, burning the house down is the best remedy for the situation.

THE YOUNG MAN. *No*, no, that's a really extreme idea, I think, so, maybe just cook something else? Maybe?

THE WOMAN. I don't know how to cook anything else. The only thing I know how to make is one thing. Marzipan.

THE YOUNG MAN. I only know how to make one thing, too. Eggs Benedict.

(a heavenly chord of music)

THE WOMAN. What did you say?

THE YOUNG MAN. Eggs Benedict.

THE WOMAN. Eggs Benedict? Eggs Benedict sounds like it can solve everything!

THE YOUNG MAN. Do you...want me to make Eggs Benedict?

THE WOMAN. Please, please do, Please, I beg you, I'll do anything – anything!

THE YOUNG MAN. Ok. Fine. Let's make a deal. You let me go take a piss and I'll make you Eggs Benedict.

THE WOMAN. Yes. No. Yes. But I can't untie you. If I untie you, you'll just leave and not make the Benedict.

THE YOUNG MAN. That's true, I might. But I definitely can't make eggs if I'm tied to a chair. Proven fact.

THE WOMAN. Wait – you just tell me what to do and *I'll* do it. And then when we're done, you get to relieve yourself!

THE YOUNG MAN. No.

THE WOMAN. Yes! This will be fun, like a cooking show! You'll be Rachael Ray and I'll be me, at home, making Eggs Benedict.

THE YOUNG MAN. No deal.

THE WOMAN. *(suddenly screaming and terrifying)* Listen to me you little bastard. Big D is coming to this house in ten God Damned minutes and if I don't have a table full of Benedict waiting for him when he arrives, I'm gonna cut your dick off and then you'll have to pee out your eye balls. You wanna pee out your eye balls, Little Bastard?

(a tension filled pause)

THE YOUNG MAN.
OKAY, YOU NEED SOME EGGS
AND SOME HAM
AND SOME BUTTER
AND ENGLISH MUFFINS

(**THE WOMAN** *is immediately filled with floating-on-air joy.*)

THE WOMAN.
I LOVE ENGLISH MUFFINS!

THE YOUNG MAN. Great.

SO SOME EGGS
AND SOME HAM
AND SOME BUTTER
AND ENGLISH MUFFINS
AND HOLLANDAISE SAUCE

THE WOMAN. Oh no!

I DON'T HAVE HOLLANDAISE SAUCE

THE YOUNG MAN. All right, all right, all right, all right.

THE WOMAN. I have... almond paste.

THE YOUNG MAN. Great.

(**THE WOMAN** *gets the ingredients and puts them on the table.*)

SO SOME EGGS
AND SOME HAM
AND SOME BUTTER
AND ENGLISH MUFFINS

BOTH.

AND ALMOND PASTE

THE YOUNG MAN.

AND YOU GOT WHAT YOU NEED TO MAKE
PARTICULARLY KICKIN' EGGS BENEDICT

THE WOMAN. So what do I do now?

THE YOUNG MAN. Well, first you gotta fry the eggs in a pan.

(**THE WOMAN** *gives him a stumped look.*)

THE YOUNG MAN.

OK, YOU GOTTA CRACK THE EGGS
THEN PUT 'EM RIGHT INTO THE PAN

(**THE WOMAN** *completes the tasks.*)

THE WOMAN.

AND PUT 'EM RIGHT INTO THE PAN

THE YOUNG MAN.

AND THEN YOU LET 'EM GET REAL HOT
YOU THINK THEY'RE GONNA BURN BUT THEY'RE NOT
DON'T WORRY, THEY'LL TURN OUT GREAT

THE WOMAN.

WHAT DO WE DO NOW?

THE YOUNG MAN.
>WE WAIT
>
>*(a moment)*

THE WOMAN. Who taught you how to make eggs?

THE YOUNG MAN. My nana.

THE WOMAN. I'm so jealous of people who got to call their grandmother "Nana."

THE YOUNG MAN. What did you call yours?

THE WOMAN. Mrs. Dodds.

THE YOUNG MAN. Yeah, well my nana died and she was, like, the one person in the world who didn't hate me, so, don't be too jealous of her. Cuz she's dead.

THE WOMAN. You remind of that sad lesbian daughter from "Roseanne." Sullen.

(An akward moment. **THE WOMAN** *thinks of what to say next.)*

THE WOMAN. What were you like in high school? Do you wanna know what I was like in high school?

THE YOUNG MAN. Nope.

THE WOMAN.
>I WAS CUTE, I WAS CUTE IN HIGH SCHOOL
>I WAS ALSO SMART
>I WAS ON THE KEY CLUB, THE GLEE CLUB AND ALSO
>I WAS GOOD AT ART
>
>I HAD A BAD BAD CASE OF
>I'LL TRY A MILLION THINGS, MASTER THEM ALL BY TWENTY
>WHICH WAS SORTA OF A PROBLEM BECAUSE
>I TRIED A MILLION THINGS, I WASN'T GOOD AT ANY
>TIME WENT BY
>AND HAIRS TURNED GREY
>AND WHAT WAS CUTE IN HIGH SCHOOL
>ISN'T CUTE TODAY
>
>AND HERE WE ARE

THE YOUNG MAN.
>AND HERE WE ARE

(a moment)

THE WOMAN. Time for *you* to share something now! Do you have a nickname?

THE YOUNG MAN. No.

THE WOMAN. I do. Miss Marzipan. Because, that's my speciality, and I thought: I'm gonna call myself Miss Marzipan, so everybody knows what I'm all about.

THE YOUNG MAN. So you gave yourself that nickname?

THE WOMAN. *(proud)* I did!

THE YOUNG MAN. Well, then it's, not – *(stopping himself)* ah.

THE WOMAN. What?

THE YOUNG MAN. Forget it.

THE WOMAN. No, What?!

THE YOUNG MAN. It's not really a nickname. A nickname is something that other people bestow on you. But you self-applied yours.

*(***THE WOMAN*** frowns.)*

THE YOUNG MAN. Which makes it a stage name.

*(***THE WOMAN*** smiles.)*

THE WOMAN. I have a stage name! Let's think of one for you.

THE YOUNG MAN. Nah.

THE WOMAN. Yes! Stage names are fun, c'mon!

THE YOUNG MAN. I really can't go take a piss now?

*(***THE WOMAN*** frowns. ***THE YOUNG MAN*** exhales loudly.)*

THE WOMAN. High school?!

THE YOUNG MAN. So –
 I WAS FAT

THE WOMAN. And?

THE YOUNG MAN.
 I WAS FAT, I WAS FAT IN HIGH SCHOOL
 I WAS REALLY FAT
 AND I WAS A SAD, MAD, ANGRY GUY YOU'LL NOTICE
 I'M STILL SORTA THAT, MINUS THE FAT

THE YOUNG MAN.
> I HAD A BAD BAD CASE OF
> NOBODY TOUCH ME OO, NOBODY TOUCH ME OO
> WHICH WASN'T A PROBLEM BECAUSE
> NOBODY WANTED TO, NOBODY WANTED TO

THE WOMAN. You were a fatty? That's adorable! How did you lose weight? Are you a huge bulimic like Ally McBeal? Like vomit jars in the closet and stuff?!

THE YOUNG MAN. I'm not a bulimic.

THE WOMAN. It's fine! I love people with eating disorders, I mean, you guys have some will power.

THE YOUNG MAN.
> SO I LOST WEIGHT, I GOT THIN IN COLLEGE
> WELL PROPORTIONED FOR MY HEIGHT

THE WOMAN. I agree – you threw up just the right amount.

THE YOUNG MAN.
> AND OF COURSE, I EXPECTED EVERY LITTLE THING
> TO BE ALRIGHT, ALL OVER NIGHT
>
> BUT I STILL HAVE A BAD, BAD CASE OF
> NOBODY TOUCH ME OO, NOBODY TOUCH ME OO
> WHICH IS A KIND OF PROBLEM BECAUSE
> NOW PEOPLE KINDA DO, SOME PEOPLE KINDA DO
>
> AND GIRLS PASS BY
> AND I SAY HEY
> AND THEY COME CLOSER
> AND I RUN AWAY
>
> AND HERE I AM

THE WOMAN. I would kill for somebody to be interested in me. People want you and you just push them away?

THE YOUNG MAN. People suck, lady. When I was fat, people were evil to me. And now I'm thin and they're all nice and stuff – it's sickening. Human beings ain't worth shit.

THE WOMAN. Some human beings are good – I truly believe that.

THE YOUNG MAN. The good ones don't care about people like me. Why would they?
ANYBODY WHO WOULD WANNA TOUCH ME
AIN'T A PERSON WORTH TOUCHING

THE WOMAN. Your stage name is Mr. Sullen! That settles it!

THE YOUNG MAN.
ANOBODY WHO WOULD WANNA TAKE ME
DON'T GO PLACES THAT I'D WANNA GO
ANY SOMEONE THINKS I'M SOMEONE
IS A MESSED UP, SCREWED UP GIRL
ANYBODY WHO WOULD WANT TO KNOW ME
IS A PERSON WHOSE PERSONAL STANDARDS ARE LOW
IS A PERSON I DON'T WANNA KNOW

THE WOMAN. You know what? You're not a pusher – you're a runner. When someone gets close, you run away. Cuz you're scared of letting people in.

THE YOUNG MAN. We've been through this. I don't get scared, I'm an apathist.

THE WOMAN. No, you're scared, just like me–

THE YOUNG MAN. *(angry)* Hey. *Fuck You*, Lady. I *choose* not to be with anyone, I'm not a loser like you who is alone because no one wants her. *(He screams and tries to break free from the chair.)* Just Let Me Go Take A God Damned Fucking Piss God Damn It! And If You're Not Gonna Let Me Take A Fucking Piss, Take The Fucking Eggs Out Of The Frying Pan So You Don't Ruin Those Too!

THE WOMAN. Oh!

*(**THE WOMAN** takes the eggs off. A horrible moment. Awkward. She puts the TV on. We hear **THE VOICE** again.)*

THE VOICE. …five minutes left to buy a brand new Top of the Line Coffin, only $33.33! Protect the corpse of you or your loved one from the elements, from the hands of children, from people-in-general! Five minutes left! Bang! Five minutes left! Bang! (**THE VOICE** *repeats this on an endless loop.*)

THE YOUNG MAN. Uh.

(**THE WOMAN** *looks at him like, "Saying something are you?"*)

Uh.

(**THE WOMAN** *mutes the TV.*)

THE YOUNG MAN. *(almost apologetic)* I yelled at you. And I was rude.

THE WOMAN. That's okay, I forgive you. *(a moment)* This is fun, isn't it? It's been so long since anyone's been to the house to converse with. *(Searching for a conversation topic)* Hey, I like your ears.

THE YOUNG MAN. Thanks.

THE WOMAN. They have the whimsy of Elf's ears, but they're not big or oafish. They remind me of autumn leaves.

THE YOUNG MAN. Thanks. *(He searches for something.)* I like your lips.

THE WOMAN. They're really big, right?

THE YOUNG MAN. Well, I like girls with big lips.

THE WOMAN. So you like *me* then?

THE YOUNG MAN. I guess.

THE WOMAN. What's your favorite color?

THE YOUNG MAN. Orange. Yours?

THE WOMAN. Green Pepper Green, what's your favorite smell?

THE YOUNG MAN. Gasoline, you?

THE WOMAN. *(fast)* Marshmallows on fire. Favorite "Spielberg" movie.

THE YOUNG MAN. *(fast)* Trick question, E.T., Favorite pizza topping?

THE WOMAN. *(fast)* Green Pepper, Favorite Song?

THE YOUNG MAN. *(fast)* "All My Little Words," favorite New York Lottery Personality?

THE WOMAN. *(fast)* Trick question, Yolanda Vega, have you ever been in love?

THE YOUNG MAN. *(fast)* No. You?

THE WOMAN. *(fast)* No.

(The fast back and forth stops. A moment.)

THE YOUNG MAN. I'm sorry I was mean to you before.

THE WOMAN. I'm sorry I kidnapped you before-before.

THE YOUNG MAN. It's cool. I don't care. So, what do you, like, do?

THE WOMAN. This and that and dot-dot-dot…

THE YOUNG MAN. I always wanted to be a writer.

THE WOMAN. Oh, sexy! That's *so* impressive.

THE YOUNG MAN. I wanted to be a songwriter.

THE WOMAN. Super sexy!

THE YOUNG MAN. Yeah.

THE WOMAN. That's *so* impressive.

THE YOUNG MAN. It was a really bad choice for me because I lose interest in things too quickly. I did write a verse of song once, though.

THE WOMAN. OH MY GOD SING IT TO ME, LET'S HAVE A CONCERT!

THE YOUNG MAN. No, no, no.

THE WOMAN. Sing it! Sing it! Sing it!

THE YOUNG MAN. I only ever sang it once before.

THE WOMAN. To who!? To your girlfriend while in the throes of passion?

THE YOUNG MAN. I sang it for my nana, actually.

THE WOMAN. The dead one! I love her!

THE YOUNG MAN. Yeah, her.

THE WOMAN. What did she have to say about it?

THE YOUNG MAN. Well, I sang it to her when she had a raging case of Alzheimer's, but I think she liked it a lot.

THE WOMAN. Sing it, Girl!

THE YOUNG MAN. No.

THE WOMAN. A true apathist would be all, "Whatever, fine, I'll sing it, I don't care." If you really don't care – you'll sing.

(**THE YOUNG MAN** *ponders this.*)

THE YOUNG MAN. Tricky. Ok. Here go. Don't laugh. Not because it'll upet me, just cuz it'll distract me.

(He prepares himself.)

THE WOMAN. Annnnnnnnnd…Action!

THE YOUNG MAN.
MONKEYS ARE COOL
BABIES ARE TOO
THEY MAKE FUNNY SOUNDS THAT SOUND SIMPLE AND NEW
THESE ARE SOUNDS THAT BELONG
IN MY TINY, SHORT LITTLE SONG

(a moment)

The monkey is my favorite animal, that's why I wrote that. Wanna hear it again?

(She nods.)

THE YOUNG MAN.
MONKEYS ARE COOL
BABIES ARE TOO
THEY MAKE FUNNY SOUNDS THAT SOUND SIMPLE AND NEW
THESE ARE SOUNDS THAT BELONG
IN MY TINY, SHORT LITTLE SONG

MONKEYS ARE COOL
BABIES ARE TOO
THEY MAKE FUNNY SOUNDS THAT SOUND SIMPLE AND NEW
THESE ARE SOUNDS THAT BELONG
IN MY TINY, SHORT LITTLE SONG

That's my song. Two people have heard it now. I just doubled it's listenership right there.

(**THE WOMAN** *takes a towel from off of the counter. She approaches* **THE YOUNG MAN**.)

THE YOUNG MAN. Yo, what are you doing?

(THE WOMAN sits next to THE YOUNG MAN and starts to wipe the blood off his forehead. He flinches.)

THE WOMAN.

DON'T BE SCARED
IT'LL ONLY HURT A BIT
EVERYTHING WILL WORK OUT FINE, FINE, FINE
YOU'RE GONNA GET OVER IT

(THE WOMAN finishes.)

THE YOUNG MAN. So, you're gonna wanna take those english muffins and lay them down on the plate, put the eggs on top and then lay the ham, then the, uh, almond paste. And there you go.

(She does this.)

Benedict.

THE WOMAN. Benedict. And that's it. Then it's done.

THE YOUNG MAN. Done.

THE WOMAN. So. *(She picks up a knife.)* I guess I'm gonna kill you now. *(a moment)* You've given me something beautiful. And now I wanna thank you by cutting your throat open.

THE YOUNG MAN. What?

THE WOMAN. Because I know it's what you really want, but you would never ask me.

(She advances towards him with the knife and puts it to his throat.)

THE YOUNG MAN. No, please, no, NO, NO, JESUS-GOD NO, PLEASE!

THE WOMAN. I'm gonna push in when I cut, that way the jugular is severed immediately and you only hurt for a couple minutes, OK –

THE YOUNG MAN. Wait, no, Stop Stop Stop.

THE WOMAN. 5,4…

THE YOUNG MAN. NO.

THE WOMAN. 3…

THE YOUNG MAN. Please!

THE WOMAN. 2!

THE YOUNG MAN. Agggggh!

(THE WOMAN stabs the knife hard into the kitchen table.)

THE WOMAN. Ha! I tricked you! Psyche! Also, you totally care about being alive!

THE YOUNG MAN. I do. That's so crazy, I do!

THE WOMAN. You care about things and you want to live. And you know that now. So there. I gave you the gift of life in return for your gift of Benedict. I think we're through.

(She loosens the ropes and immediately starts finishing up the benedict. She sets the table. **THE YOUNG MAN** *jumps up, he's out of breath.)*

THE WOMAN. Now be gone with you, Big D's gonna be here any second! You know what? I think I'm gonna be fine without you.

THE YOUNG MAN. And I'm just gonna pee in a bush.

THE WOMAN. Great!

THE YOUNG MAN. Great!

THE WOMAN. OK!

THE YOUNG MAN. So, uh, bye?

THE WOMAN. Yes, bye –?

THE YOUNG MAN. Matthew! Matthew Fry. Is my name.

(He holds out his hand to shake.)

THE WOMAN. Jenny. Veccharelli. Is mine. Goodbye, Matthew.

MATTHEW. Goodbye, Jenny.

(A moment. They looks at each other. They shake hands. He leaves. We are now outside the house. **MATTHEW** *looks around. He sees a* **SLICK DUDE** *taping something to the mailbox at the edge of* **JENNY**'s lawn. **SLICK DUDE** *notices* **MATTHEW**.)*

SLICK DUDE. Hey, there Young Man, are you – do you know Jenny?

MATTHEW. Uh, yeah.

SLICK DUDE. Oh, sweet, uh – well, listen I had mentioned that I might stop by for a drink or something, but there's a bunch of us and we're going to party or something, I think –

MATTHEW. Is that your limousine?

SLICK DUDE. You're a funny guy. It is. It's mine. Like, I actually own it. I don't rent it, if that's what you're thinking. There's money in computers, my short little friend – Crazy money.

*(A **SLUT** and **ANOTHER SLUT** stumble over. They are high and generally messed up.)*

A SLUT. Big D, c'mon baby, let's go!

ANOTHER SLUT. *(Waves at **MATTHEW**)* Hiiiii.

BIG D. Ah, tell Jenny that I'm sorry I missed her and tell her "next time," K, Buddy?

MATTHEW. I'm her son. I'm not her buddy, I'm her son.

BIG D. I didn't know Jenny got knocked up. Good for her, somebody loved her enough to, ya know, ha.

MATTHEW. Lots of people love her.

*(**THE SLUTS** laugh.)*

She's totally successful. We're very happy.

A SLUT. Come On, Big D, that coke's not gonna snort itself!

ANOTHER SLUT. *(to the other **SLUT**)* Hiiii.

BIG D. All right, duty calls, I guess!

MATTHEW. Hey – Jenny was telling me, and I'm sorry your wife died. Lots of people in my family have died, too.

BIG D. Yeah, well – I got over it. It's easy to forget when you're a billionaire.

*(**BIG D** splits with his **SLUTS**. The sound of laughing and a limo pulling away. **MATTHEW** reads the note that was taped on the mailbox.)*

MATTHEW. "Dear Jenny, Big D Wuz Here. Maybe you should've been better to me in high school. Fuck You. Love, Big D."

(*MATTHEW crumples the note. A moment. MATTHEW looks around. He goes back into the house. MATTHEW walks into the kitchen. The chair with the ropes on it still sits at the table.*)

MATTHEW. Yo.

JENNY. You came back! Why?

MATTHEW. He's not coming.

JENNY. Who?

MATTHEW. Big D.

JENNY. Of course he is!

MATTHEW. I just saw him outside. He said he was sorry but he couldn't come.

JENNY. Big D is here?!

(*JENNY rushes to the window.*)

MATTHEW. He was here but he left in his limo. He said he was sorry but he couldn't come.

JENNY. No! I don't believe you.

(a moment)

MATTHEW. He said that he was in too much pain from his wife dying to start dating again.

JENNY. Oh. So maybe he wants to reschedule?

MATTHEW. Also, he said that he's gay now.

JENNY. *(sad)* Oh. Well. There goes that then.

MATTHEW. Yeah.

JENNY. Thanks for coming back to tell me. You didn't have to do that.

MATTHEW. I wanted to.

JENNY. You did?

MATTHEW. I wanted to.

JENNY. You wanted to?

MATTHEW. I did.

JENNY. Well, thanks.

MATTHEW. So, I guess I'll go now?

JENNY. Alright.

MATTHEW. Unless –

JENNY. What?

MATTHEW. Nothing.

JENNY. No, what?

MATTHEW. I thought maybe, uh –

JENNY. Do you want to –?

MATTHEW. Maybe –

JENNY. Oh.

MATTHEW. As long as you don't –

JENNY. I don't mind!

MATTHEW. It's just…it's a lot of Eggs Benedict. I can't stand to see Eggs Benedict go to waste. Huge part of my personality. Don't like to be egg-wasteful.

JENNY. Funny.

MATTHEW. Yeah.

(**JENNY** *sits at the table. She motions for* **MATTHEW** *to sit.* **MATTHEW** *chooses the chair with the ropes. He sits.*)

MATTHEW. Uh –

JENNY. What?

MATTHEW. Would you mind –?

JENNY. Oh. Not at all. You go right ahead. What ever dot-dot-dot…

(**MATTHEW** *wraps the rope around his body. He sighs in contentment.*)

JENNY.
 THANK YOU SO MUCH
MATTHEW.
 YOU ARE WELCOME
JENNY.
 THANK YOU SO MUCH

MATTHEW.
>YOU ARE WELCOME
>
>*(They begin to eat their Eggs Benedict.)*

MATTHEW. How do you like them?

JENNY. I think they're the most delicious eggs I've ever had.

MATTHEW. They are! Is this weird that we're hanging out?

JENNY.
>WE'RE JUST TWO PEOPLE TALKING
>WE'RE JUST TWO PEOPLE TALKING
>WE'RE JUST TWO PEOPLE TALKING TO EACH OTHER
>WHAT'S WEIRD ABOUT

JENNY & MATTHEW.
>TWO PEOPLE EATING
>TWO PEOPLE SMILING
>TWO PEOPLE TALKING

MATTHEW. Could I actually use your bathroom for real?

JENNY. I'd be honored.

>*(**MATTHEW** goes into the bathroom. **JENNY** looks around the table and smiles. We hear the sound of **MATTHEW** pissing.)*

JENNY & MATTHEW. *(The ultimate sigh of momentary contentment.)* Ahhhhhhhhhhhhhhhh.

The End

MINI-MUSICAL #3

THE PROCESS

CHARACTERS

JOE
THE GIRL BEHIND THE COUNTER
LADY CUSTOMER

and **The Enablers:**
MOM
A FAN BOY
MICK

(**JOE** *is sitting at a table in a Dunkin Donuts, drinking coffee.* **THE GIRL BEHIND THE COUNTER** *sort of stares at him.* **JOE** *is oblivious to this. He sits alone, talking to himself. He is having the time of his life.*)

JOE. January 16th. 2010. 9:02pm. I am going to write a musical. More specifically, I am going to write a Great musical. As I am a great musical theater writer. It's something that they just can't teach you in school. Other guys, they're scared to do what I do. They write about the French Revolution or Peter Pan. But not me, sir! I get right in there, I do! I write from myself and luckily, I'm a pretty interesting guy. But what to write This time. Ah. There's the rub. I've got so many options. I write what I love.
I LOVE DUNKIN DONUTS, MOVIES, BLOOD, AND BOURBON
I LOVE HIGH SCHOOL PROMS, AND CRAZY MOMS, AND
   ANYTHING SUBURBAN
I LIKE TO WRITE SO EVERYBODY CAN SEE
ALL THE CRAZY SHIT THAT LIVES INSIDE ME
BUT MOST OF ALL I LOVE THE DUNKIN DONUTS

(in a James Lipton "Inside the Actors' Studio" Voice) Thank you so much for agreeing to be interviewed today.
(in a normal voice.) No problem, Mr. Lipton.
(James Lipton) The only other musical theater writer ever to be on "Inside The Actors' Studio" is Mr. Stephen Sondheim.
(normal) I'm not familiar with his work. Hahaha!
(Lipton) Hahaha!
(normal) Seriously, it's an honor to be here.
(James Lipton) So tell me – why Dunkin Donuts? Most writers would be too untruthful to work in a place as pedestrian as this Dunkin Donuts!

JOE. *(cont.) (normal)* Well, I'm not most writers. I write about the everyman – about people who don't usually get shows written about them.

(James Lipton) How brave.

(normal) Quit embarrassing me, you!

(James Lipton) So, what's the new one gonna be about, m'boy?

(normal) Funny you should ask! I was just thinking about that myself –

THE GIRL BEHIND THE COUNTER. Hey!

(**JOE** *is ripped out of his little fantasy world. He immediately deflates and looks a bit fatter/uglier.*)

JOE. Yeah?

THE GIRL BEHIND THE COUNTER. Hiiiii.

(**JOE** *smiles. Waves. Buries himself in his yellow legal pad and writes furiously.*)

THE GIRL BEHIND THE COUNTER. You want a muffin? More coffee?

(**JOE** *stops writing.*)

JOE. I think I'm allowed to sit in here if I buy one every hour and it hasn't been an hour yet.

THE GIRL BEHIND THE COUNTER. *(sweetly; with a smile)* I'm not kicking you out. I'm making a conversation.

JOE. Oh. *(Back down to the pad.)*

THE GIRL BEHIND THE COUNTER. Mr. Writer, what are you writing?

JOE. It's, uh, a musical.

THE GIRL BEHIND THE COUNTER. Like "Spider Man?"

JOE. *(Almost responds for real. Decides not to. Not worth it.)* Yes.

THE GIRL BEHIND THE COUNTER. What's it about?

(**JOE** *looks up. He thinks about this. Suddenly, we are back in his fantasy world.*)

JOE.
>ROCK AND ROLL AND GUYS WHO FEEL UNWORTHY OF ATTENTION
>WITH PERFECT RHYMES AND STRUCTURAL CLIMBS THAT SCREW WITH CONVENTION
>THEY'RE A CORNUCOPIA OF STONERS AND NERDS
>ABOUT PORN AND DOPE AND FOUR LETTER WORDS
>THAT'S WHAT THEY'RE ALL ABOUT
>MOTHERFUCKER, YEAH
>THAT'S WHAT THEY'RE ALL, UH –

THE GIRL BEHIND THE COUNTER. Hey!

(**JOE** *is snapped back to reality.*)

THE GIRL BEHIND THE COUNTER. *(Waving)* Hiiiii.

JOE. I don't know what it's about yet.

THE GIRL BEHIND THE COUNTER. Well, let's think, we'll come up with something together!

JOE. Ha, no no no.

THE GIRL BEHIND THE COUNTER. You should write something about aliens, like Little Mr. E.T., I just love him.

JOE. E.T.?

THE GIRL BEHIND THE COUNTER. Yeah! Know him?

JOE. Uh, yeah, that's one of my favorite movies actually, but, it's really not helpful to me right now.

(**THE GIRL BEHIND THE COUNTER** *smiles, inspects him.*)

THE GIRL BEHIND THE COUNTER. You don't have a girlfriend, do you?

JOE. No. I'm between mates.

THE GIRL BEHIND THE COUNTER. Does that mean gay?

JOE. No. It's just a funny thing to say.

THE GIRL BEHIND THE COUNTER. Why is that funny?

JOE. I can't explain the rules of comedy to you, you either find me funny or you don't.

THE GIRL BEHIND THE COUNTER. I find you funny, just not the things you say to me.

JOE. Uh, I feel like you are taking an active interest in me tonight. Why are you taking an active interest in me tonight?

(*A moment.*)

THE GIRL BEHIND THE COUNTER. Because I have been studying you, Mr. Writer. You have been coming here for years scribbling on that pad and I wanna know. What are you writing?

JOE. (*Trying to sweetly brush her off.*) Eh, I'm not sure.

THE GIRL BEHIND THE COUNTER. Tonight's my last night, you know. You're my Last Customer Ever. It's past closing. I'm staying open for you.

(**JOE** *looks up.*)

JOE. Much obliged?

(**JOE** *goes back to writing in his pad.*)

THE GIRL BEHIND THE COUNTER. (*A moment. Then she pounces.*) What are you writing?, lemme see!

JOE. No, no, no, don't!

(**THE GIRL BEHIND THE COUNTER** *and* **JOE** *struggle with his pad. She reads it. He is so embarrassed.*)

Those are my notes. Then I turn them into dialogue. It's my process.

THE GIRL BEHIND THE COUNTER. (*reading from the pad*) "A writer is sitting at a table in Dunkin donuts, drinking coffee. The Girl Behind The Counter sort of stares at him." Oh my god, you're writing about the Dunkin! Nobody cares about the Dunkin!

JOE. Some people do. I truly believe that.

THE GIRL BEHIND THE COUNTER. "The Writer has been attracted to her for years and years" – Ah! – "and she's finally talking to him." Why'd you write this?!

JOE. Give that back, c'mon.

THE GIRL BEHIND THE COUNTER. Wait, if you've been hot for me for years, why wouldn't you just ask me out?! Why'd you just write about it?

JOE. *(embarrassed)* I'm a writer. This is my process. I take things in my life and then I transmogrify the feelings into a heartfelt piece of theater.

THE GIRL BEHIND THE COUNTER. Your mouth is a volcano of bullshit right now.

JOE. My mouth is not that.

THE GIRL BEHIND THE COUNTER. Let's recap.

(**THE GIRL BEHIND THE COUNTER** *gets up and paces. She is a detective trying to get to the bottom of a great mystery.*)

You've been coming here for years. You've always been attracted to me. Yet you've never done anything about it. You just bury yourself in that Yellow legal pad. That's unhealthy. Worse than Donuts, even.

(**JOE** *writes in the pad.*)

JOE. That's a funny line.

THE GIRL BEHIND THE COUNTER. Oh My God, Look! You're doing it now! Look look!

JOE. What?

THE GIRL BEHIND THE COUNTER. Writing, not talking! I'm sorry it to say it, but I think you're a pussy.

(a moment)

JOE. Did you just call me a pussy?

THE GIRL BEHIND THE COUNTER. I did.

JOE. You're not allowed to do that. You're The Girl Behind The Counter.

THE GIRL BEHIND THE COUNTER. I'm just trying to help you fix you.

JOE. I don't need fixing, I'm a perfectly happy guy.

THE GIRL BEHIND THE COUNTER. Sounds to me, Joe, like you hide behind your words. For someone who writes from his own experience, I don't think you experience much at all.

JOE. That's a shitty thing to say to me.

THE GIRL BEHIND THE COUNTER. Don't shoot the messenger.

JOE. I need to begin my writing process now, thanks.

THE GIRL BEHIND THE COUNTER. Of course you do. Because you don't live your life. You write it.

JOE. Leave me alone!

THE GIRL BEHIND THE COUNTER.
WHERE YOUR BALLS AT?
WHOA
WHERE YOUR BALLS AT?
JOE
I DON'T THINK YOU EVEN KNOW ANYMORE

JOE. Oh, I know lady. My boys are Huge, OK?

THE GIRL BEHIND THE COUNTER. Then use them! Listen to those little voices in your head. The ones that say: "Stop writing. Start living."

JOE. Yeah, the voices in my head don't really say things like that.

(**MOM** *appears. She glows with Beauty and is the perfect suburban housewife.*)

MOM. Joseph – there's my handsome boy! What's your new show going to be about?

JOE. I don't know, mom! Something wonderful, I bet!

MOM. Oh Goodie-Goodie-Gumdrops! And can it be performed in Connecticut? I've always wanted to go to Connecticut!

JOE. Sure can, Mom!

THE GIRL BEHIND THE COUNTER. Who are you talking to?

MOM. And after the show is over I'll take you out for a nice Italian dinner and I'll protect you from people-in-general!

JOE. See, they're actually pretty supportive. They make me feel special!

THE GIRL BEHIND THE COUNTER. You're not special!

JOE. Excuse me, I've changed people's lives.

(A FAN BOY in a Wicked T-Shirt enters.)

A FAN BOY. Your music has changed my life.

JOE. They've told me so.

A FAN BOY. I was going to kill myself but then your song got me into the University of Michigan.

MOM. When I listen to your songs, I forget about how empty my life is.

A FAN BOY. And now everything's fine!

THE GIRL BEHIND THE COUNTER. Stop getting distracted! We need to work on something here.

JOE. I've gotta write!

MOM.
> I LOVE IT WHEN YOU WRITE YOUR SONGS, JOE
> I LOVE IT WHEN YOU WRITE YOUR SONGS

JOE. They love it when I do this!

A FAN BOY.
> I LOVE YOU WHEN YOU WRITE YOUR SONGS, JOE

BOTH.
> ONLY WHEN YOU WRITE YOUR SONGS

JOE. *(to THE GIRL BEHIND THE COUNTER)*
> SEE YOU CAN TRY TO
> GET IN MY WAY OR CHOP ME UP, MAYBE
> SAY THAT I'M NOT OKAY AND DROP ME, YUP, BABY
> CAN ENDEAVOR ALL DAY TO STOP ME, WHUP, HEY
> BUT LA, LA, LA, LA, LA, I'M NOT LISTENING GO AWAY

THE ENABLERS.
> WE LOVE IT WHEN YOU WRITE YOUR
> LOVE IT WHEN YOU WRITE YOUR
> LOVE IT WHEN YOU WRITE YOUR SONGS

GIRL.
> STOP!

THE ENABLERS.
> ONLY WHEN YOU WRITE YOUR
> ONLY WHEN YOU WRITE YOUR
> ONLY WHEN YOU WRITE YOUR SONGS

GIRL.
STOP!
You've got Too Many Enablers up there, Young Man.

JOE. "The Enablers." That sounds like a band name.

GIRL. They are preventing you from living your life.

JOE. They are so not.

A FAN BOY. I just want to you to keep writing musicals and never do anything else!

MOM. And then you'll never find a girl and you'll never have babies and never leave us ever again!

MOM & A FAN BOY. Yay!

THE GIRL BEHIND THE COUNTER. They are fueling you to keep being a pussy.

(**MICK JAGGER** *appears.*)

MICK JAGGER. Joe.

JOE. Hey, Mick.

MICK JAGGER. Hey, Joe! Man, I love those musicals you write. So funny and truthful and irreverent. I've often said, if the Rolling Stones were a musical theater writer, they'd be you.

JOE. Thanks, bro!

THE GIRL BEHIND THE COUNTER. Who are you talking to now?

JOE. My bestie, Mick Jagger.

THE GIRL BEHIND THE COUNTER. Mick Jagger is not your bestie.

MICK JAGGER. What does bestie mean?

THE GIRL BEHIND THE COUNTER. You need to tell him, Shut The Fuck Up!

JOE. You can't say Shut The Fuck Up to Mick Jagger!

THE GIRL BEHIND THE COUNTER. Sure you can, watch – Hey, Limey – Shut The Fuck Up and Stop Messing With My Friend's Head.

JOE. *(a little giddy)* Are we friends?

THE GIRL BEHIND THE COUNTER. Christ, listen, there's no way the pressure they are putting on you feels good.

JOE. I don't care!

THE GIRL BEHIND THE COUNTER. You think just ignoring the problem is going to help?

JOE. Yes!

>   *(***THE GIRL BEHIND THE COUNTER** *grabs* **JOE** *by the ear and twists it, hard.* **THE ENABLERS** *yell a little.)*

THE GIRL BEHIND THE COUNTER. *Where Are Your Balls, Joe?!*

JOE. They're in my pants!

THE GIRL BEHIND THE COUNTER. *Where Are Your Balls, Joe?!*

A FAN BOY. Oh, she's fierce!

THE GIRL BEHIND THE COUNTER. *Balls, Balls, Balls!*

(She lets go of his ear.)

MOM. All this testicle talk is in very poor taste.

JOE. Hey, now you "Christ, listen!" I'm a smart guy. I understand what you are telling me. I'm not experiencing my own life because I'm too busy writing, which is easy to do as I am scared of rejection and completely seduced by the adoration of others.

MOM. Well, you're a young man!

JOE. Exactly! I've got time to participate in my own existence. Later.

THE GIRL BEHIND THE COUNTER. Your time is up.

JOE. It might not be… *(making quotation mark fingers)* "healthy," or whatever, but I just wanna write. It's not hurting anyone. And I'm sorry I keep making quotation mark fingers. I actually really hate quotation mark fingers.

THE GIRL BEHIND THE COUNTER. Joe, those fuckers are gonna live in your head forever.

THE ENABLERS. Yeah!

THE GIRL BEHIND THE COUNTER. And sure, they're building you up now, but mark my words, they'll turn devil on you.

MOM. That woman is positioning you against me.

A FAN BOY. She makes me sad – I'm gonna cut myself.

THE GIRL BEHIND THE COUNTER. Stop hiding in your writing! If you don't, there's gonna be hell to pay and I won't be here to help you.

(He looks at his pad. A huge moment.)

THE ENABLERS.
>PICK UP THE PENCIL
>PICK UP THE PAD
>GO, GO, GO, GO, GO, GO, GO, GO
>WE LOVE YOU WHEN YOU WRITE YOUR SONGS, JOE
>WE LOVE YOU WHEN YOU WRITE YOUR SONGS
>ONLY WHEN YOU WRITE YOUR SONGS, JOE
>ONLY WHEN YOU WRITE YOUR SONGS

JOE.
>YEAH, YEAH, YEAH YOU CAN TRY TO
>GET IN MY WAY OR CHOP ME UP, MAYBE
>SAY THAT I'M NOT OKAY AND DROP ME, YUP, BABY
>CAN ENDEAVOR ALL DAY TO STOP ME, WHUP, HEY
>BUT LA LA LA LA LA LA
>LA LA LA LA LA LA LA LA
>LA LA LA LA LA LA LA LA
>I'M NOT LISTENING GO AWAY

THE ENABLERS.
>HEY! WE LOVE IT WHEN YOU WRITE YOUR
>LOVE IT WHEN YOU WRITE YOUR
>LOVE IT WHEN YOU WRITE YOUR SONGS

JOE.
>YEAH!

THE ENABLERS.
>LOVE IT WHEN YOU WRITE YOUR
>LOVE IT WHEN YOU WRITE YOUR
>LOVE IT WHEN YOU WRITE YOUR SONGS

*(***JOE** *and* **THE ENABLERS** *dance like happy babies! They are having a ball!* **THE GIRL BEHIND THE COUNTER** *just shakes her head. This is all so sad to her. Suddenly, the door opens. Record scratch.)*

LADY CUSTOMER. Hey!… You open?

(Everyone is startled and immediately stops dancing. **JOE** *shrinks back to his pad. Phew, that was a close one. And then he notices who just walked in. A* **LADY CUSTOMER***. She looks at the Donuts.* **JOE** *sees her, but she does not see him. He recognizes her.)*

JOE. Oh, holy shit.

*(***LADY CUSTOMER** *turns around and* **JOE** *flinches and covers his face so she doesn't see him. No dice.* **LADY CUSTOMER** *walks towards* **JOE***. Is it who she thinks it is? Is it who she thinks it is? Oh, shit. Yup. That's him.)*

LADY CUSTOMER. Hey.

*(***JOE** *doesn't respond.)*

Hey you.

JOE. Me?

LADY CUSTOMER. Yeah. It is you.

JOE. Hi.

LADY CUSTOMER. I know you.

JOE. Ha, uh, OK.

LADY CUSTOMER. We went to school together.

JOE. Oh, crazy, awesome, yeah, uh –.

LADY CUSTOMER. Don't pretend like you don't know my name.

JOE. Ah, you know, I'm so bad with names.

LADY CUSTOMER. Yeah, you are.

JOE. I'm sorry, I just don't really remember. Yikes almighty.

LADY CUSTOMER. Don't you pull that cute shit with me. That cute shit doesn't do One God Damn thing for me.

JOE. OK, whoa, like – uh, I don't remember your name. I'm sorry. Are you Megan? Megan, right?

LADY CUSTOMER. My name is Jenny. Veccharelli. You God Damn asshole.

JOE. Jenny! Ah! Ah! How you been?

JENNY. Yeah, you know what?, not so good, OK? You know why, not so good? Cuz you put my name in your fucking stupid asshole musicals and my mother is at the Food Basket and Mr. Dodds comes up to her and says: I heard that Jenny kidnapped someone!

JOE. Oh my God, really?

JENNY. She started crying. In the Food Basket. I kidnapped someone, Mr. Dodds heard. Or how about when I was at the reunion, and Margaret Murphy says – "So are you and Joe, like, in Love? Are you his muse, are you his Uma Thurman?" And I'm all, "Margaret I haven't the slightest idea what you're talking about," and she goes, "Oh, well Joe wrote all these musicals about you. Everybody knows." Do you know what that feels like?

JOE. Flattering?

JENNY. Not so much, Joe, it's more like being raped. Like being raped by, oh, I dunno, an invisible werewolf. It is creepy and scheevy and rape-ish.

JOE. I can see that you are vaguely upset.

(There is a change in **JENNY**.*)*

JENNY. Oh, you have no idea. You. Have no clue.

JOE. I don't –

JENNY. You know what? Forget it.

JOE. What?

(a moment)

JENNY. We were supposed to end up together.

JOE. What are you talking about?

JENNY. In high school. You never asked me to the prom. You didn't have the balls. You liked me, right?

JOE. I write musicals about you.

JENNY. Great. That's great. But do you know what would have happened if you had just asked me? *(a moment)* Our life together was supposed to be perfect.

WE GO TO THE PROM AND WE GET MARRIED TO EACH OTHER

> WE HAVE THREE CHILDREN AND THEY LOVE US SO MUCH
> I'M A REALLY GOOD MOM, I'M NOT AT ALL LIKE MY MOTHER
> AND WHEN THINGS GET SCARY I AM CALMED BY YOUR TOUCH

JOE. *(to* **THE GIRL BEHIND THE COUNTER***)* This can't be for real.

THE GIRL BEHIND THE COUNTER. It is.

JOE. I'm sorry, Jenny, but I don't think that type of life – *(runs out of words)* I'm a writer.

JENNY.

> WE HAVE ALL OF THAT AND YOU'RE ALSO JUST THE MOST SUCCESSFUL WRITER
> MORE FULFILLED AND CONTENT THAN YOU ARE RIGHT NOW
> AND WE EAT OUR MEALS IN THE KITCHEN WITH OUR CHILDREN
> AND THE SUN'S JUST BRIGHTER
> SOMEHOW
>
> THEN ONE DAY WE WALK UPSTAIRS TO OUR BEAUTIFUL BEDROOM
> AND WE DIE IN EACH OTHER'S ARMS AT THE VERY SAME MOMENT
>
> THEN ONE DAY WE WALK UPSTAIRS TO OUR BEAUTIFUL BEDROOM
> AND WE DIE IN EACH OTHER'S ARMS AT THE VERY SAME MOMENT
>
> THEN ONE DAY WE WALK UPSTAIRS

*(***JOE** *becomes hypnotized by the life he could have had.)*

JENNY & JOE.

> TO OUR BEAUTIFUL BEDROOM
> AND WE DIE IN EACH OTHER'S ARMS AT THE VERY SAME MOMENT
>
> THEN ONE DAY WE WALK UPSTAIRS TO OUR BEAUTIFUL BEDROOM
> AND WE DIE IN EACH OTHER'S ARMS AT THE VERY SAME MOMENT

JOE. That is beautiful.

JENNY. It could've been.

JOE. I'm sorry I ruined that for you. I never meant to.

(**JOE** *retreats to his pad.*)

JENNY. Well. You ruined it for yourself. (*She notices he's writing.*) And you're still doing it, look at this, you're still doing it!

(**JENNY** *rips the pad away from* **JOE**. *She reads from it.*)

"The real JENNY V. walks into the Dunkin Donuts and I feel like I'm gonna piss my pants…" Oh. (*She reads on.*) "And we have three children and they love us…" Ew.

JOE. Those are my notes, you can't read those!

MOM. Yeah, stop bothering my child.

(**JENNY** *flips madly through the pages.*)

(*to* **MOM**) "My mother's voice blares in my ear. I know she means well, but does she realize how suffocating her love is?"

MOM. The fuck you say?

(**JENNY** *throws the pad on the ground, and* **THE ENABLERS** *scramble to pick it up. They read from it.*)

JENNY. This can't continue.

A FAN BOY. (*looking up from the pad*) You called me "pathetic?"

JOE. It's called artistic license!

A FAN BOY. It's called being a dick wad.

THE GIRL BEHIND THE COUNTER. Not so adoring anymore, are they?

JOE. Whatever. They just get like this sometimes.

MICK JAGGER. (*looking up from the pad*) Am I really too old to be wearing leather pants?

THE GIRL BEHIND THE COUNTER. This is gonna get ugly.

MOM. I loved you. I supported you. And this is how you repay me?

JOE. No, I love you too, I just get upset with you sometimes and it comes out in the writing.

A FAN BOY. If you have a problem with me, why don't you just tell me to my face like a real man?

JENNY. And why do you even think that anybody cares about these stupid mundane things that you write about?

A FAN BOY. He's a poor man's Tom Kitt!

JOE. Be quiet!

THE GIRL BEHIND THE COUNTER. *(Biblical; huge) These are the consequences of a life not lived.*

MICK JAGGER. I'll never be too old to wear leather pants, let's fuck him up.

JOE. I don't know what to do!

JENNY. His self-indulgence is apocalyptic. He needs to be stopped.

A FAN BOY. Let's cut his hands off!

THE ENABLERS. Yeah!

JOE. Gimme my pad!

THE GIRL BEHIND THE COUNTER. Stop writing start living!

(**JOE** *grabs his pad.*)

JOE. I need to get away!

THE GIRL BEHIND THE COUNTER. *You need to face these monsters! Look at them! C'mon!*
WHERE YOUR BALLS AT, JOE?

JOE.
IT'S SO HARD TO REMEMBER, OH

THE GIRL BEHIND THE COUNTER.
NO!
WHERE YOUR BALLS AT, JOE?
WHERE YOUR BALLS AT, JOE?

THE ENABLERS. *(overlapping)*
I'M NOT GONNA LET YOU WRITE THAT SONG, JOE
I'M NOT GONNA LET YOU WRITE THAT SONG
I'M NOT GONNA LET YOU WRITE THAT SONG, JOE
I'M NOT GONNA LET YOU WRITE THAT SONG

(**JENNY** *runs over to* **THE ENABLERS**. *A microphone stand appears.* **JENNY** *grabs it.*)

MICK JAGGER. Ladies and Gentleman, Put Your Hands Together for "Jenny and the Enablers!" 1-2-3-4…

(**JENNY** *turns into a total rock star. Overpowering rock concert lighting! Pyro!*)

JENNY.
ROCK AND ROLL AND GUYS WHO FEEL OF UNWORTHY OF ATTENTION
WITH PERFECT RHYMES AND STRUCTURAL CLIMBS THAT SCREW WITH CONVENTION
IT'S IMITATION WITH A PLASTIC HEART
IT'S MASTURBATION DISGUISED AS ART

MICK.
IT'S SO LAME!

MOM.
IT'S A SHAME!

A FAN BOY.
WHAT A CROCK!

JENNY.
WHOA, THAT'S WHY WE'RE GIVING YOU THE BLOCK

(**JENNY** *and the* **ENABLERS** *crowd around* **JOE** *until they are screaming in his face. He tries to hold his ears and write.*)

THE ENABLERS.
YEAH, THAT'S WHY WE'RE GIVING YOU THE BLOCK
YEAH, THAT'S WHY WE'RE GIVING YOU THE BLOCK

THE GIRL BEHIND THE COUNTER.
FACE THE CRAZY HONEY, DON'T JUST HIDE

THE ENABLERS.
WE'RE GIVING YOU THE BLOCK

THE GIRL BEHIND THE COUNTER.
USE THE FUEL YOUR LITTLE WORDS PROVIDE

THE ENABLERS.
WE'RE GIVING YOU THE BLOCK

THE GIRL BEHIND THE COUNTER.
>TO TAKE SOME ACTION AND TO TAKE THE RIDE
>THE ONLY WAY TO ADVANCE
>TAKE A STAND, TAKE A CHANCE OR
>C'MON GIVE US AN ANSWER TO
>WHY DO YOU ONLY WRITE YOUR LIFE, JOE?

THE ENABLERS.
>WHY DO YOU ONLY WRITE YOUR LIFE, JOE?

ALL.
>WHY DO YOU ONLY WRITE YOUR LIFE?

(Dead silence. **JOE** *looks at everyone. Gulp.)*

JOE.
>I WISH I WAS THE TYPE OF GUY
>THE TYPE WHO COULD SAY WHATEVER HE FELT
>BUT I FIND THAT I – WHENEVER I TRY
>MY BRAIN GOES BLANK AND MY WORDS MELT
>
>SO I WRITE IT ALL DOWN
>AND I FILTER IT THROUGH
>AND FOR ME THAT'S THE KEY
>THEN IT'S EASY TO SEE WHAT I THINK ABOUT YOU
>HOW I THINK ABOUT YOU
>HOW I FEEL ABOUT YOU
>OO-OO-OO-OO
>OO-OO-OO-OO

Jenny – I'm sorry.

THE GIRL BEHIND THE COUNTER. Why?

JOE. *(to* **THE GIRL BEHIND THE COUNTER***)* Cuz in high school –

THE GIRL BEHIND THE COUNTER. Tell her.

JOE. Cuz I loved you kinda. But I never told you that. Because I thought you would laugh at me because I was a fatass. Ah. I was *scared* of you. So I turned you into a lady who kidnapped me and tried to kill me. I wrote a musical where I got to ask you to the prom three times. Jenny, if I use your name in my writing, it's because I wanted to ask you to the prom in high school and I didn't.

MOM. You know, I think I like it better when he turns his feelings into a song.

A FAN BOY. When he just says it like this it's boring.

MICK JAGGER. Let's exit.

(**THE ENABLERS** *exit.*)

JOE. I'm sorry I never just spoke to you. But I'm gonna make things right. Now.

(**JOE** *revs up.*)

JENNY
JENNY
JENNY, I GOT SOMETHING –

JENNY. *(cutting him off)* No. This isn't a musical. This is real life and I will not let you rewrite this into a heartfelt piece of theater. I'm sorry – I just won't. *(huge pause)* And that... was the last *line* I will ever say to you.

(**JENNY** *exits.*)

THE GIRL BEHIND COUNTER. Real life. It's not easy.

(**JOE** *looks at his pad. He wants to pick it up so badly.*)

JOE. This is probably where I'd hunker down and channel my feelings into some heartbreaking writing.

THE GIRL BEHIND THE COUNTER. But that's not what you did before with Jenny. You actually talked to her.

JOE. Yeah. And that didn't turn out well.

THE GIRL BEHIND THE COUNTER. Exactly. but that's the way it goes. You can't always rewrite the bad shit. You just gotta experience it and keep on.

JOE. So what do I do now?

THE GIRL BEHIND THE COUNTER. You're doing it, I think.

JOE. Yeah. I'm not writing. I'm talking. I'm just... experiencing.

(A moment.)

Is this enough? Is this, like, the completion of my arc?

THE GIRL BEHIND THE COUNTER. Don't Be Mr. Writer.

JOE. Sorry. I'm just confused here, what was I supposed to learn from all of this? *(Working through it.)* I think that if this conversation we're having ends up in a musical, then I am a total failure.

(**THE GIRL BEHIND THE COUNTER** *makes a "That might be true" face.*)

JOE. Or or or or, maybe as long as I don't let the writing of this conversation get in the way of it actually happening, its all ok. Right?

THE GIRL BEHIND THE COUNTER. Honestly, honey, I don't know what the fuck you're talking about anymore.

JOE. Sorry. Forget it. What I really meant to say was… The Girl Behind The Counter… would you like to sit down and have some coffee with me?

THE GIRL BEHIND THE COUNTER. Finally. Something I understand.

(**THE GIRL BEHIND THE COUNTER** *sits at the table with* **JOE.**)

Let's drink up. I've got all the time in the world.

JOE. Me too, I guess.

(**THE GIRL BEHIND THE COUNTER** *goes to say something. Stops herself. Takes a moment. Continues.*)

THE GIRL BEHIND THE COUNTER. If you do turn this into a musical? Don't put my name in it. Keep that for yourself.

JOE. That'll be easy.

THE GIRL BEHIND THE COUNTER. Why?

JOE. Cuz I don't know your name. What is it?

(**THE GIRL BEHIND THE COUNTER** *thinks long and hard. She thinks long and hard. She goes over to him and whispers her name in his ear.*)

JOE. Good name.

THE GIRL BEHIND THE COUNTER. Thanks.

JOE. This rocks.

THE GIRL BEHIND THE COUNTER. I think it's kinda weird.

JOE.
>WE'RE JUST TWO PEOPLE TALKING
>TWO PEOPLE TALKING
>TWO PEOPLE TALKING TO EACH OTHER
>WE ARE TWO PEOPLE TALKING
>ACTUALLY TALKING
>TWO PEOPLE TALKING TO EACH OTHER
>
>WHAT'S WEIRD ABOUT

JOE & THE GIRL BEHIND THE COUNTER.
>TWO PEOPLE TALKING
>TWO PEOPLE TALKING
>TWO PEOPLE TALKING TO EACH OTHER

JOE.
>WHAT'S WEIRD ABOUT
>
>*(We see* **NELSON** *and* **JENNY**. **MISS MARZIPAN** *and* **THE YOUNG MAN**. *Each caught in their own "Two People Talking" moments.)*

ALL.
>TWO PEOPLE TALKING
>TWO PEOPLE TALKING
>TWO PEOPLE TALKING TO EACH OTHER
>
>WE ARE TWO
>TWO PEOPLE STUMBLING
>TWO PEOPLE SIGHING
>TWO PEOPLE FUMBLING
>TWO PEOPLE TRYING
>
>TWO PEOPLE GIVING
>TWO PEOPLE LIVING
>
>TWO PEOPLE TALKING THROUGH THE NIGHT

JOE.
> AND THAT, BABY, THAT IS THE REWRITE
>
> (**JOE** *throws his pad down. He looks around. S'all good, man. S'all good.*)
>
> YEAH

ALL.
> YEAH

The End

AUTHOR'S NOTE

The following is an interview with Mr. Iconis, conducted by Mrs. Thurser, a fictional character featured, briefly, in *ReWrite*:

MRS. THURSER: Hello, Joe. Before we begin, I'd like to thank you for creating me.
JOE: Don't mention it.
MRS. THURSER: So, tell us a little bit about how *ReWrite* began.
JOE: Well, I wrote "*Nelson Rocks!,*" the first part of *ReWrite* at the NYU-Tisch Grad Musical Theater Writing Program as a stand alone piece. I always had a fondness for the show, but because of its unusual structure, I felt that it shouldn't be expanded - it seemed like a perfect little twenty-five minute experience. A few years later, I thought I would write a couple other short pieces and do all three in concert. This wasn't gonna be a musical, however. Absolutely not. This was simply going to be an evening at the theater featuring a bill of three, unrelated mini-musicals. The only thing they were to share were an author credit and an abbreviated runing time. I had no intentions of writing the thing you are currently reading. It just sort of happened. The characters took hold and before I knew it, I had written three short musicals that all ended up being about the same thing.
MRS. THURSER: You confuse me. As does this show.
JOE: Well, that's kind of the idea. I hope that the show catches its audience off guard. I like that people walk into the theater thinking they are seeing a triple feature of unrelated short musicals, and by the time they get to the end of part II, its very clear that something altogether bizarre is going on.
MRS. THURSER: That displeases me. I like knowing exactly what I'm going to see before I see it.
JOE: I'm sorry to disappoint you.
MRS. THURSER: That's alright. I'm used to disappointment. Back to your play (if you can even call it that.) There's a character in it named Joe and he is a musical theater writer. Is this supposed to you?
JOE: I don't know. I guess it is.
MRS. THURSER: Isn't that a little, ya know. Stupid?
JOE: It might be. To be honest, I don't think it's important that anyone know that the character of "Joe," is supposed to be me. I think the important thing is that Joe is a musical theater writer who wrote the first two mini-musicals. In the New york production, I played on-stage piano, and there was another actor playing the character of "Joe."
MRS. THURSER: Does that mean that you have to be in every production of this show?
JOE: Not at all! In fact, I'm excited to see productions that don't involve me at all.

MRS. THURSER: Me too. So, I don't understand what happens in between the mini-musicals. Surely, there are missing parts that were left out of this edition of the script on account of human error.

JOE: No. I'm not really sure what happens in between the three parts. I think it has to do with whatever your interpretation of the show as a whole is. In the New York production we had these elaborate transitions that gave the impression that we were seeing the inner working's of a writer's mind. There were projections of images referenced in the show and insane music and pre-recorded dialogue. In a subsequent workshop, we didn't use any transitions at all, it just went from one to the next. The first time we ever did the show, I had Abraham Lincoln be the M.C. for the evening and do stand-up comedy in between the acts.

MRS. THURSER: Baffling. Next question. Was there really a Jenny Veccharelli?

JOE: [Answer removed.]

MRS. THURSER: Incendiary. So, tell me- what does it all mean?

JOE: What does what mean?

MRS. THURSER: The show? What am I supposed to feel at the end?

JOE: I don't know! I couldn't begin to tell you what you're supposed to take away from this show. I know what I take away from it, but I'd never be so bold as to impose that on you. I think there are big questions in the show that purposely go unanswered. I'd love for people to come up with their own answers and explanations and theories about what it all means. I think at its heart, this show is about a man who is learning to live his life, not just write it. Personally, I don't think he's a success by the end, but I think he's on the road to success.

MRS. THURSER: So, it's a happy ending?

JOE: I dunno. Sort of? Depends on how you look at it.

MRS. THURSER: I only like things with neat, happy endings.

JOE: I see. Well, I'm sorry, Mrs. Thurser, I'm afraid I just can't give you one of those.

MRS. THURSER: Oh no?

[MRS. THURSER pulls out a huge knife and plunges it deep into JOE's heart. A small, bloody tear falls from his eye as he collapses into a pile of the floor. MRS. THURSER then goes home to her husband, who has just returned from the war. They lovingly embrace as the Publisher's Clearing House van pulls up. All join hands and sing a song about hopes and dreams and light, as the curtain falls.]

ABOUT THE PLAYWRIGHT

Joe Iconis is the author of *Bloodsong of Love: The Rock 'n' Roll Spaghetti Western, ReWrite, The Black Suits* (book co-written by Robert Maddock), *The Plant That Ate Dirty Socks, We The People,* and *Things To Ruin.* He is the recipient of an Ed Kleban Award, and a Jonathan Larson Award, and is a two-time Drama Desk nominee. He is a Long Island native and a proud graduate of NYU (Steinhardt and Tisch's Graduate Musical Theater Writing Program.) Joe is a great fan of Robert Altman, Dolly Parton, The Rolling Stones, and the family of artists he frequently collaborates with.

OTHER TITLES AVAILABLE FROM SAMUEL FRENCH

THE PLANT THAT ATE DIRTY SOCKS

Joe Iconis
Based on the Book by Nancy McArthur

TYA, Musical Comedy / 4m, 2f / Interior

Michael's closet has exploded! At least, that's what it looks like, with all the baseball cards, heaps of crumpled paper, clothes strewn about, and piles of smelly, dirty socks everywhere! It's the battle of the bedroom, as his younger brother (and roommate) Norman fights to keep his spotless territory from the invasion of Michael's mess. But that was before the appearance of their pet plants! Michael's pile of stinky socks disappears faster than you can say "My goodness, what an enormous plant," as Mom and Dad struggle to keep the bizarre botanical wonders under wraps...What would the neighbors think? A fun-filled musical, based on the popular book series, celebrating individuality, brothers working together, and the most disgusting plant food ever!

"FOUR STARS! Just as successful children's shows once spawned junior versions of themselves so, perhaps, are musical-theater favorites ready for their own era of kid-size knockoffs...Iconis can be proud of the bouncy pop tunes and clever rhymes he has devised for this occasion: It's a rock-'em–sock-'em little score!"
– *Time Out New York*

"*The Plant That Ate Dirty Socks* is sure to please thousands of elementary schoolers."
– *Variety*

"Joe Iconis has created a musically exuberant score and playful lyrics that fit the story... this new "family rock" musical has silly charm to spare!"
– *Curtain Up*

SAMUELFRENCH.COM

www.ingramcontent.com/pod-product-compliance
Lightning Source LLC
Chambersburg PA
CBHW070647300426
44111CB00013B/2310